600 DECORATING TIPS AND FINISHING TOUCHES

Tessa Evelegh

600 DECORATING TIPS AND FINISHING TOUCHES

HERMES
HOUSE

This edition is published by Hermes House

Hermes House is an imprint of Anness Publishing Ltd, Hermes House, 88-89 Blackfriars Road, London SE1 8HA, tel: 020 7401 2077; fax 020 7633 9499; info@anness.com

© Anness Publishing Ltd 2003

A CIP catalogue record for this book is available from the British Library.

Publisher: Joanna Lorenz
Managing Editor: Helen Sudell
Project Editor: Joanne Rippin
Designer: Nigel Partridge
Production Controller: Steve Lang

Publisher's Note: Fruit and vegetables used for display purposes should not be consumed.

10 9 8 7 6 5 4 3 2 1

contents

introduction

Our home, more than anything else, is an expression of ourselves. It is the place where we can relax, and be comfortable with who we are. As well as comfy chairs, restful beds and plentiful storage for quick tidying up, it can provide us with an avenue for expression of who we are right now. Just as you wouldn't dream of wearing the same clothes year in, year out, there is no reason why your home should look the same from one Christmas to the next, but there is a problem. Replacing a piece of furniture, or going-the-whole-hog and redecorating, is an expensive business, and one that was overcome in the past by simply not changing anything at all until it had worn out. Times have changed, and interiors have become much more fashion-driven, but thankfully, there is a lot we can do and buy to create whole new looks without completely discarding what went before, and indeed, who would want to? We are all a combination of past and present, and to completely discard our own past would be to throw away a whole dimension of our lives. The trick is to create an easy-to-live-with blank canvas in our homes on to which we can paint and repaint as trends and our own styles

evolve and change. Once the basic design is complete, there is plenty of scope to dress a room up or down or to create a new ambience by changing one or two elements or by introducing something new that will influence the whole interior. Even if you don't want to repaint a whole room you can update the look, just by painting one wall. Alternatively, you could keep to the same colour family but add an interesting paint technique to make a feature of one wall. Be careful in choosing which wall you want to feature, it has to have a naturally inbuilt sense of importance. It may already incorporate an architectural feature, such as a fireplace, or it may be opposite a window where the natural light will enhance a special colour, or you may want to make a statement on a landing or hallway.

Even without the colour element, paint finishes can make a very clear fashion statement. Smooth paint more or less had a monopoly from the late 1940s to the 1980s when more interesting textures and finishes from past centuries were rediscovered. The fashion for increasingly distressed looks dominated until, in the 1990s, plain, dead-flat finishes became more de rigueur. Now, we have a wide

choice, giving us flexibility to use what suits both our houses and ourselves. Old furniture can be updated quickly and easily with a fresh coat of paint or a new finish.

A change of window treatment in any room is another dramatic way to bring a new mood. Full curtains, even with simple headings, make a room look warm and cosy with a traditional feel, but exchange these for Roman blinds, and the look will become elegantly classic with a modern edge. Even the choice of smaller accessories, such as cushions, can have an effect on the ambience of a room. In the living room as well as using cushions, you will find you can make an immense difference with throws. Shake one out over the sofa for an instant impact on the colours and patterns in the room. In the bedroom, the endless choice of designs for bed linens means you can create a completely new look every time you change the sheets. In the dining room, the table dominates the room, so you can alter the whole atmosphere by changing the table linen and tableware. In the bathroom, a new set of towels create a whole new colour scheme. Even the lotions and potions you choose and the way

you package and display them can have an impact on the look of the whole room. The impact of kitchens is most affected by the colour and style of the cupboards, especially if you keep everything behind closed doors. If you prefer open shelves, you can display favourite casseroles, teacups, vases and storage jars, using them to bring instant colour and style to the space.

Outside, gardens, patios and decking are very much part of the home and increasingly the style of the home infiltrates the garden. Paints and stains on garden sheds, fences, trellises and furniture bring all-year colour to outside spaces. Pots, containers and garden accessories can mirror in-home detailing, and decorative lighting brings sparkle to our outdoor space. The increasing popularity of eating in the garden means there is plenty of scope for dressing the patio for dinner.

These are all just glimpses of the hundreds of ideas you will find in the pages of this book. It is a treasury of inspiration that can make real changes in your home through attention to details, giving you the scope to evolve ideas that reflect your own style and your personality.

living rooms

More than any other room in the house, the living room is for leisure. It is used for relaxation – reading, watching television, listening to music and welcoming visitors. There are times when it has to be on show, yet it doesn't want to be too precious. In short, the living room has a lot to live up to. The answer is to choose an unfussy basic scheme, and then concentrate on details such as window treatments, accessories, lighting and flowers, which can be changed easily with the seasons or to suit different occasions.

white inspiration

Smart, timeless and loved by architects and designers, white on white always looks good, whatever your style. White is calm, light-reflective and offers few distractions, but there are many different whites to choose from, ranging from cool chalky shades to the warm creamy white of a swan's wing or a white rose. In a shady room with windows that face a garden, white walls will reflect the plants, taking on a green tinge, yet in a sunny room, stark brilliant white could be just too bright. Look at the huge range of whites visible in natural settings, and don't be afraid to use a mixture of different tones in a single room.

TEXTURAL CONTRAST

In a room with no colour, texture can be used to add an element of contrast. Here, a fluffy cushion and rug set against smooth upholstery introduce understated visual interest to an all-white room.

▲ Light-reflective white accentuates form and texture, as this delicate white papier-mâché bowl demonstrates.

▼ Frothy white lilac blossom gives a dramatic textural element in a white room.

PURE FORM

Accentuate strong lines with white. Here, a square white chair complements the stark geometric shape of a modern fireplace. Minimalist rooms such as this one need little embellishment, so keep the accessories simple. Just three mind-your-own-business plants (*Soleirolia*) planted in sharp geometric pots that are in keeping with the fireplace do the trick. They grow naturally into perfect orbs, contributing a little geometry of their own.

A TOUCH OF COLOUR

Two standard box (*Buxus*) trees, clipped into globes, have been brought in from outdoors for impact and to emphasize the purity of the rest of the room. Plants are an excellent way to introduce colour into white rooms, because, being organic, they don't make a design statement that could date quickly. However, as box trees do not thrive indoors, they should be used only for a particular function or a limited period, then returned to the garden.

warming colour

A room decorated in warm colours can lift the spirits and stimulate the brain, inspiring good conversation and creating a party mood. In hot countries, such as Mexico, South-east Asia and India, the bright natural light makes a virtue of fabulous hot colour clashes such as fuchsia pink with orange, while cooler countries have traditionally favoured warm crimson and any of the yellows. Earthy browns and sepias also have a gentle warmth that works well in colder climates.

STARS AND STRIPES

Terracotta lends a warm cosy feel, but using it to paint a whole room could be overpowering. You can soften the effect by applying alternate stripes of terracotta and pale coral. Adding silver stars to the stripes creates an altogether brighter look. Try this idea for a whole room, or if you prefer simply paint the stripy effect on the wall opposite the window to reflect and magnify incoming light, while colouring the other walls in solid terracotta for a warm shadowy effect.

WARM SPECTRUM

This sumptuous interior combines all the basic hues from the warm end of the rainbow. Reds, oranges and yellows sit cheek by jowl creating a hot feel worthy of an Arabian Nights' film set. It is all the more effective for the confidence with which the colours are combined. They are all strong deep tones that are comfortably hot together, uninterrupted by pale colours that would visually jump out at you. Old-gold upholstery on the sofa, the gilt mirror and the wooden table bring the lightest relief, while the green skirting (base) board adds just a touch of cool.

EARTH TONES

Echoing the natural tones of our outside environment, earth colours can be confidently mixed and matched. Because they are at one with the natural world, earthy schemes are often very beautiful. Here, the warmth of untreated wood teams with muted browns and sandy hues to create a natural, soothing colour scheme that is easy to live with.

SPICY MIXES

For a truly exotic and warm scheme, try blending the glowing colours of Eastern spices. Here, the soft tones of turmeric, cinnamon and cardamom have been successfully combined to reproduce an exciting look that is reminiscent of North Africa. There are plenty of other subtle tones in the spice palette that could work well together.

EXTROVERT COMBINATION

Seven sari lengths, in yellows, reds and oranges, were the inspiration for this flamboyant scheme. Given top tabs, they make wonderful sheer curtains, and the light filtering through them has the effect of blending the colours. Pink and red cushions add clashing hues that work well together within the context of a hot scheme such as this one.

ELEGANT WARMTH

The soft tone of plaster pink can make a good starting point for a warm colour scheme. Here, it is teamed with a deep indigo curtain and a smart tan chair.

details that count

Whether you want to add new finishes to lend extra depth and interest to the living room, or simply to revive a tired surface, this is the time to pay attention to detail. A new paint technique, a little gilding or a painted border can all lend personality to a room. Don't skimp on the preparation. The surface to be treated must be smooth, dry and sound, otherwise whatever you paint or apply will soon begin to peel or flake, and will quickly look tatty.

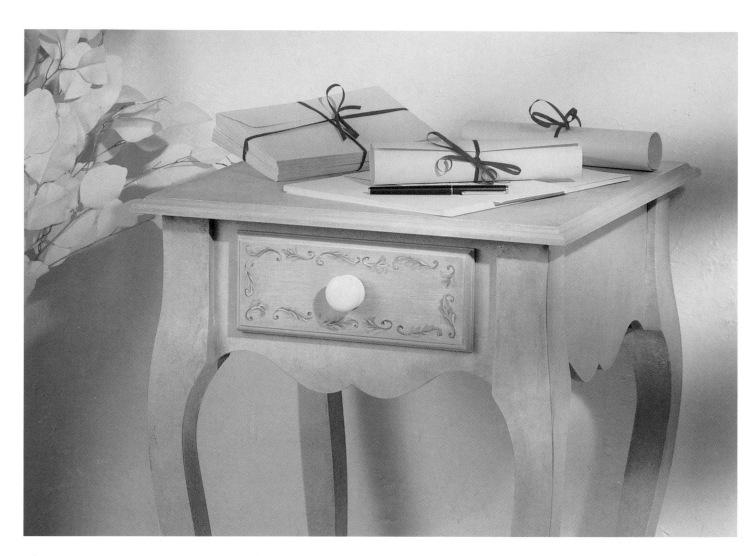

CLASSIC SCROLLS

Painted furniture can be given a new lease of life with the addition of some classic scroll detailing. Start by painting a scrolling leaf design around the edge of a drawer front, or down the legs of a small occasional table. Paint the leaves in pale green and allow to dry. Then, using a fine artist's brush, pick out the leaf veins in mid-green. When dry, add white and yellow highlights to the leaf design, still using the fine brush. Once the paint is thoroughly dry, seal the surface with a coat of acrylic varnish to protect it against knocks and scratches.

GRAINED DOOR

Strongly textured combed graining is achieved by mixing wall filler with sky-blue emusion (latex) in the proportions of 25 per cent filler to 75 per cent paint. Paint this mixture on to the door, working on a small section at a time. While it is still wet, use a wide-toothed comb to comb in the lines, following the grain. Once the paint is thoroughly dry, apply a thin coat of emulsion; here lime green was the colour. Leave to dry overnight, then sand back for a surprisingly subtle effect. Finally, seal the door with two coats of acrylic varnish, allowing it to dry between coats.

DECORATIVE ESCUTCHEON

Most modern door escutcheons are fairly plain, being of white plastic, brass, stainless steel, glass or translucent Perspex. Here is a clever technique for adding interest to a clear glass door plaque. It has the advantage that it can be changed very quickly and easily whenever you want to redecorate the room.

1 Cut a rectangle of cardboard slightly larger than the plaque. Fix the cardboard to a block of wood, using masking tape. Spray the card with several thin coats of gold paint. When the paint is completely dry, remove it from the wood block. Lay the plaque centrally on the gold card and draw a pencil line around the plaque.

2 Arrange motifs or pictures on the gold cardboard panel, then glue them in position, using PVA (white) glue diluted with an equal amount of water.

3 Cut out the gold cardboard around the pencil line using a craft knife. Paint it with several layers of clear water-based acrylic satin varnish. Allow each coat to thoroughly dry before applying the next.

4 Place the door plaque over the decorated panel and fix them both to the door usings screws and a screwdriver.

AN ORIGINAL FRIEZE

To make an architectural frieze, photocopy drawings from out-of-copyright books available from art shops. Reduce or enlarge them to suit. Cut them out, paste on to the back of a wide wallpaper border and varnish before fixing in position.

GILDING THE LILY

Gilded fleur-de-lys bring an unusual decorative touch to a feature wall. Try this in alcoves either side of a fireplace, on a wall opposite a window to reflect the light, or behind a special piece of furniture.

window treatments

The way windows are dressed contributes hugely to the overall style of a room. Drapes, pelmets, swags, valances and other elaborate headings are generally considered classic, and the fuller and more gathered they are, the more traditional. Nowadays, they are usually hung on plastic curtain rails that are designed to be hidden by the heading or a pelmet. Wooden curtain poles traditionally have a country feel; the curtains hang either on curtain rings or by loops or ties. Modern window treatments are generally simpler. Less fabric is used, and, very often, simple panels are hung at windows from fine metal curtain poles using metal curtain clips. These dispense with much of the stitching, yet the overall effect is nonetheless sleek and smart.

SWAG AND TAILS

This formal curtain treatment became very popular in England during the Regency period at the end of the eighteenth century, and still has classic appeal. It looks most elegant on tall windows.

ADD A SIMPLE PELMET

Plain cream drapes and a matching wavy-edged pelmet create an elegant classic look. The pale cream linen gives a light effect, so that, even when closed, the curtains do not make a heavy contrast against the white walls. A pelmet is a useful device in situations where the windows are rather low, as it adds visual height without blocking out any precious natural light. Pelmets can also be used to visually even out discrepancies in height where a room has several windows at different levels.

COUNTRY APPLIQUE

A painted wooden curtain pole and tied heading lend a charming country look to this cottage-style window. The feel is reinforced by the use of country-look fabrics – natural-coloured linen and cheerful gingham appliqué. The denim detailing lends a contemporary look. At the hem of the curtain, willowy flowers have been appliquéd in matching gingham and denim to give the impression they are growing up the curtain, while co-ordinating with the heading and ties above. An extra long pole has visually enlarged the window and so helped to improve the proportions of the room.

TIMELESS STYLE

Within the context of a classic room, this fine metal curtain rod with shepherd's crook finials makes for a smart modern window treatment. The curtains are hung on curtain clips that slide on rings along the rod. This discreet fitting works for all sizes and shapes of window as it doesn't dominate the curtain or border panel. Small windows, however, would need simple, unembellished panels to visually enlarge the proportions. These curtains are elegantly tall, and so can take more detailed panels, such as these simple mitred corners and a deeper top section that mimics a valance.

decorative sheers

Muslins, voiles and nets create a gentle mood by tempering bright daylight, and can also be used creatively to enhance the look of windows. Overlooked city-dwellers may prefer to hang sheers in order to protect their privacy, as well as to disguise views that are less than glorious. Sheer fabrics need to be chosen in conjunction with the main curtains or blinds, although – in summer, at least – they may be all you need to dress a window prettily.

CUSTOMIZE SHEERS

There are endless sheers and voiles available to buy – and not necessarily in curtain fabric departments. Dress fabrics have huge choices of organzas and organdies, and Asian markets offer fine silks and saris in a myriad colours as well as muslins in creams and whites. Sheers look best when they are not over-gathered, otherwise you risk the boudoir look. However, they can be swagged, draped and otherwise hitched up, and endlessly customized with trimmings. Here, a simple bobble edging makes for an interesting window treatment.

▲ *Applied decorations can transform the simplest of curtains. This seashore theme was achieved simply by stitching seashells in position. String ties threaded through eyelets and tied on to a bamboo pole make a delightful no-sew heading. If you collect your own shells, drill a fine hole through each one to take the thread. Alternatively, dismantle a ready-made shell product for ready-drilled shells.*

◄ *Applied decorative motifs, such as these ribbon flowers, work well on sheers because they are set off by light shining through the curtain.*

TEXTURE AND PATTERN

Plain natural linen curtains can be given extra textural interest by drawing out threads to make squares and stripes. It is easiest to draw threads on loose weave fabrics with strong fibres, but before attempting it on the full length of the curtains, try it out on a sample piece of fabric to make sure it will work and to see the finished effect. Once all the threads had been drawn on these curtains, square mother-of-pearl buttons were added to reflect the light and emphasize the pattern. The tabbed heading echoes the width of the drawn-thread stripes, and is also finished with buttons.

SIMPLEST STYLE

If you need to protect your privacy but nets are just not your style, hang sheer panels at the window. They are easy to hang on the simplest of rods and curtain clips. Quick to put up, they are also quick to get down again when they need to be washed. Since during the day it is lighter outside than in, these sheer panels prevent passers-by from prying, while hardly restricting any light from coming into the room. In the evening, when you switch on the lights, the reverse is true, so you will need to draw thicker drapes or a screen across the window to guarantee privacy.

▼ *No-sew sheer swags are easy to do. Buy a long length of fabric that is twice the height of the window plus twice the width then drape it generously around a curtain pole. The main sheer is attached to a rod behind the swag.*

window decoration

There are many decorative elements that can enhance main curtains, blinds or panels, all adding to the overall effect of the window treatment. Windowsills, if you have them, are a great advantage, as they can be used for simple arrangements of flowers or accessories. If you're not too overlooked, these accessories can even become the window treatment itself, accentuated by back lighting from the great outdoors.

FLORAL SCULPTURE

If you have a contemporary look with blinds instead of curtains, reinforce the theme of diffusion with agapanthus and papyrus blooms, which are perfect for moving everything upwards and outwards. To match the simplicity of the room's design stand the blooms in single, matching, plain glass vases. This lends flexibility, as you can change the floral arrangement with the seasons. Choose twiggy or simple sculptural flowers and foliage to retain the same overall personality of the arrangement.

STREAMS OF LIGHT

If you need to maximize the light streaming into a dark room, such as a basement, try this trick. Hang three sheer panels, knotting the ends so the bottom window panes are barely covered, then stand glass vases containing sculptural flowers on the windowsill for interest. Coloured sheers add extra detail. Used in combination, they work like an artist's palette, blending into a new hue where the curtains overlap.

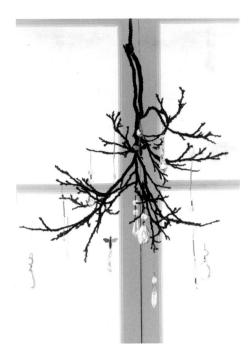

CRYSTAL WINDOW HANGING

A pretty hanging of twigs and light-reflecting chandelier drops is all you need to make a feature of an elegant window that is not overlooked. Search out an attractive branch with plenty of curved twigs to complement the feminine feel of the droplets. Attach the droplets with silver thread or fisherman's wire.

FEATURE EDGES

Edges are always on view, even when curtains are drawn back, and you can focus these for the simplest, most effective decoration. These delicate shells look particularly pretty when the curtains are gently swagged.

GLITTERING BEADS

Strands of coloured beads are used here to soften a stark window, rather than to protect privacy or provide warmth. The larger droplets and heart-shaped beads lend emphasis to the inverted V-shaped profile. The glassy theme is extended into the windowsill arrangement.

TIE BACKS

Details in strong hues, such as crimson, deep pink or russet, can introduce temporary or even seasonal changes to an all-white room. These tie-backs were quickly made by fixing ribbons to a tassel base. The celebratory effect is perfect for a summer party.

decorative mosaics

Architectural detailing, such as flooring, fireplaces, tiles and mosaics, need to be chosen with care. They are difficult and expensive to change, so you are likely to be living with them for some time. When selecting tiles and mosaics, bear in mind the colour of the grouting, which can make a profound difference to the finished result. When you are choosing flooring or wall finishes, take samples home and place them where they will be situated so you can see them in the correct light at different times of the day.

A MOSAIC HEARTH

Mosaics bring colour and decorative detail to an elegant marble fireplace. Mainly in blue, it is only the mosaic's border that is patterned, which saves the hearth from becoming over-fussy. The same colour grout has been used for all the hearth, illustrating how it looks with differently coloured tiles. In the border, it contrasts with the white tiles, accentuating them and adding to the geometric pattern. It can be tempting to set off tiles with contrasting grout, especially if they are specialist ones, such as round mosaics. But beware of too much contrast, as the effect could be dazzling. If in doubt, leave the tiles fixed but ungrouted for a while, giving you time to ponder the alternatives.

HOW TO: APPLY MOSAIC

1 Cover any bare wood with wood primer and allow to dry, then draw your design.

2 Mix up tile adhesive according to the manufacturer's instructions and 'butter' it on to the back of each piece of mosaic before fixing in position. Allow the adhesive to dry completely.

3 Mix up the grout according to the manufacturer's instructions, adding colour if required. Wearing rubber gloves, work it between the mosaic pieces using your fingers. Use a washing-up brush or a toothbrush to work the grout off the surface of the mosaic and into the gaps.

4 Leave to dry, then polish the surface of the mosaic with a soft cloth.

SHAPING UP

The tiny tiles in mosaic work make it the perfect medium to use on intricate shapes. The curvy frame on this mirror is accommodated by a random blend of pale green mosaic tiles, giving it an interesting, elegant look. The finished piece is infinitely feminine and, although its curves are almost rococo in style, it makes the perfect accessory for a stark geometric fireplace. Pieces like this can change the whole personality of a room, lending it architectural importance.

MIXED MEDIA MARQUETRY

This modern minimalist coffee table would have been unequivocably plain without the mosaic panels, which have been inset marquetry-style into the polished wood surface. It is a clever individual piece in that the strength of the design will always make the table a focal point of the room, yet the multicoloured mosaic allows for future radical changes to the decor of the room itself. Set in a different colour scheme, the coffee table would certainly take on quite a different personality.

DOUBLE IMPACT

Make a statement with matching mirror frames positioned symmetrically, on either side of a fireplace for example. Here, two simple mirrors have been given matching mosaic frames using the same tiles but arranged in a different pattern. The matching pair technique can be repeated with almost anything – lamps, chairs, candlesticks, etc. With this treatment, matching pairs take on a feeling of solidity and permanence rather than a transitory feel that accessories can give.

fresh looks for furniture

It's easy to give a new lease of life to old wooden chairs, table and cabinets, which can be stripped down and given a range of new finishes. So if you have acquired a disparate collection following junk shopping sprees or raids of granny's attic, why not give them fresh style with some creative paintwork, gilding or mosaic tiles? The key is to select pieces that have a pleasing shape to start with. Choose items that look good and well-balanced from every angle: incongruous proportions will become all too obvious once a piece has been given its new look. Avoid furniture with too much extraneous embellishment, as this can make the refurbishment tricky.

PAINTED TABLETOP

Old tabletops can be transformed with a lively painting. First make sure the surface is sound, clean, dry and has an undercoat. Use emulsion (latex) for the design as it is more manageable than oil-based paint. When this is thoroughly dry, protect the surface with hard-wearing acrylic varnish.

PAINT CHAIRS TO MATCH

This chair has been given a finish resembling Chinese lacquer, using glossy black paint, with details picked out in gold and a gold-stencilled motif. This kind of paintwork helps to unify non-matching items of furniture. Give several odd wooden chairs the same treatment, and they will look like a set.

DISTRESSED CHAIR

Battered old metal garden chairs often come in very pretty shapes, and with a little effort can take on a whole new life indoors. An easy way to refurbish them is to spray with a specialist metal paint, which not only covers rust, but cures it too and can be subsequently re-coated with any paint suitable for metal.

▼ *The pretty proportions of this Gothic-style corner cabinet really come alive with gilding. The blue base coat gives the piece a delightful individual look with a timeless, yet contemporary, feel.*

▼ *When given the gilding treatment, this little French-style side table makes a pretty living-room feature.*

THE GOLDEN TOUCH

Gilding can transform many pieces of tired old furniture. Despite the glitzy results, gilding is not a difficult technique to do. Choose well-proportioned pieces and prepare the surface meticulously before painting on two coats of emulsion (latex), following the manufacturer's instructions. Once dry, apply water-based size and leave for 20–30 minutes before applying aluminium Dutch metal leaf. Rub with a soft cloth to remove excess leaf, then rub back the gilt on high-wear areas, such as corners, to reveal the base coat, using steel wool dipped in methylated spirits (methyl alcohol). Seal with water-based flat varnish. The bold, broadly-striped upholstery gives this Louis XV-style chair a zany updated look.

tailored treatments

Dress up tired old side chairs or mismatched sets to give them fresh new life. As well as disguising incongruous shapes or battered profiles, the covers can be matched with the décor. If you make a set for each season, you can ring the changes to suit the weather. Make them trim and tailored in elegant linen mixes, or a little more relaxed in heavy cottons or chunky weaves. It is best to choose a natural fibre such as pure cotton or linen as these are usually machine-washable (check the care label before buying), so in the event of spills and stains, they can be whipped off and put into the washing machine, ready to go back on the next day.

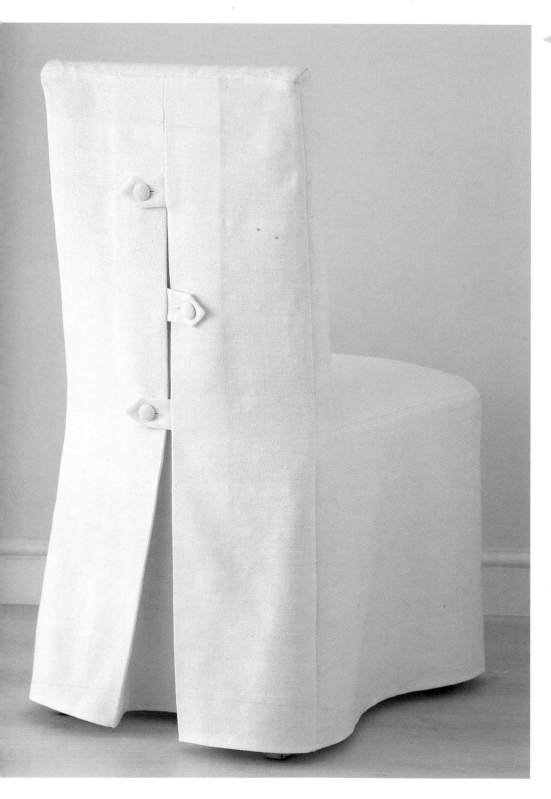

CHAIR TRANSFORMATIONS

New cotton covers instantly revive tired chairs. This stylish cover has taken several tips from the fashion catwalk, with a smart box pleat at the back to make it easier to get on and off. It is made in white, firm weave, crisp crease-resistant cotton. The large covered buttons and bold pointed loop buttonholes reinforce the tailored look of the chair, and give the finished design an unfussy elegance.

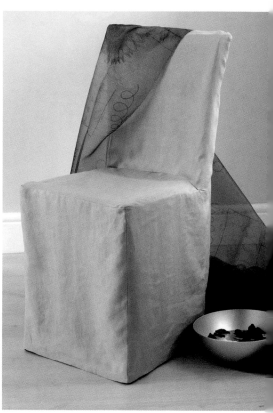

▲ *Slip-on covers like this look best on side chairs with tall slim proportions, as the overall effect is more elegant. They can take on a distinct fashion feel to suit different occasions. Dress them up at party times with a length of coloured organza, draped over the chair back.*

▲ Use dye to achieve your favourite colour. It works brilliantly on machine washable, pure cotton loose covers. Here, a brightly coloured beaded panel has been appliquéd on to the back for extra interest.

◄ This tightly upholstered chair has been given a deeply scalloped valance for an elegant feminine look in keeping with the curvy wooden legs.

► Slip-on covers in brightly coloured stripes give this tub chair a strong new contemporary look.

instant upholstery

If complicated sewing skills aren't one of your greatest talents, take easier options. Revive your living room furniture with clever tie-ons and cover-ups. They will update the room without the expense of buying a new sofa or chairs, or paying for new upholstery, and they are an easy way to make use of fabrics in the latest colours and textures. Another way to give upholstery a new look is to dye loose covers in the washing machine. This works best on natural fibres such as pure cotton or linen, especially light-coloured ones. Try it with your old upholstery, or, if you are looking for new pieces and can't find the colour you want, seek out inexpensive chairs with removable white cotton covers, which you can dye to team with your scheme.

TIE-ON COVERS

You can freshen up sofa and chair arms with tie-on covers. As well as being a brilliant way to update upholstery, they are handy for disguising chair arms that have become grubby over the years. The idea of loose covers is not new; the Victorians used antimacassars (extra cloths for chair backs and arms to protect against soiling by macassar hair oil). Nowadays, instead of necessarily matching the existing chair covers, you can use the tie-ons as a design element by choosing a contrasting fabric for a whole new updated look.

▼ *Tie-ons are an easy solution for anyone who can use a sewing machine. Cut the main fabric to size, then stitch on satin binding and organdie ribbon ties.*

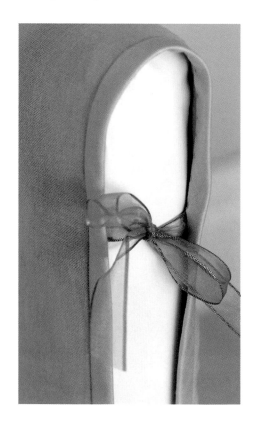

COVER UP

If a tatty old coffee table is detracting from the rest of the décor, throw over a cloth for a fresher, more unified look.

PRETTY STAMPING

Print your own designs on to old chair covers or inexpensive plain fabrics. The easiest way to do this is to stamp on the design using fabric paint and a ready-made stamping block available from decorating stores. Wash the fabric first, as the paint will only adhere to clean dry materials. Do this even if the fabric is new, as you will need to remove any dressings. Stamp the motifs on randomly, as here, or in a more regimented design, following the lines of the chair.

DREAMY DRAPES

Whether you are re-upholstering in a hurry, or trying to co-ordinate disparate furniture, this has to be the quickest solution. You will need a large piece of fabric for each chair – pure white cotton sheets are one possibility. Drape it around the chair and bring the ends round to the back, then tie in a huge knot. The key is to tie a neat knot, otherwise your room could end up looking like the place has been mothballed under dust sheets (drop cloths). Take your time and re-tie the knots if necessary. This is a clever solution for large special celebrations where, perhaps, unmatched chairs are being brought from various parts of the house but you would prefer a more cohesive look. To add an extra flash of colour and create a flamboyant party look, tie a huge bow, in a firm fabric such as metal-shot organdie, through the back.

cushion style

In a sitting room, cushions (pillows) are the most versatile of accessories. Their style has great influence on the feel of the whole room, yet they can be swapped around or re-covered easily to change the mood or update the interior. They can also be used to add accent colours, teamed with the main colour of the room, frilled for a feminine touch or piped to look city-smart. Make them big and squashy for a comfy, inviting look, or small and neat for an elegant one.

ADD STYLE WITH TRIMS

Bobbles, tassels, fringing and fraying add interest to plain cushion covers, while even the fastenings can become a feature. Choose ties for a casual look, a row of tiny buttons with rouleau loops for a touch of couture, or large bold buttons in contrasting colours for a witty modern feel. Bold inset panels or stripes look good in modern apartments. Big, squashy square cushions spell comfort, but, by their sheer size, their colour can have a big impact on the interior. Neater, tailored and shaped cushions generally give a city look. This group of cushions includes plenty of interesting detail: ties, buttons, piping, ringing, and even fun embellishments made from string, lend each cushion a completely different personality. If you want to mix several different styles like this, use fabrics that tone to ensure the end result isn't over-fussy.

▶ *Give cushions a nautical look by inserting brass rivets at regular intervals around the edges and then threading them through with white piping cord. The choice of thick linen as the fabric and the blue and white colour scheme reinforces the maritime theme.*

FORMAL ARRANGEMENT

A co-ordinated set of cushions will give your sofa a new look. This classic, plain, cream-coloured sofa has been livened up using a boldly panelled throw and teaming it with cushions that are in equally strong colours. The opulence of the colours and fabrics is tempered by the strict formality of the arrangement.

CONTRAST PANEL

In a spare, contemporary setting, a plain black cushion becomes a focus of interest with the addition of a contrasting appliqué square. The classical script adds a discreet element of pattern, yet its subtle colouring stops it looking fussy. Make a cover like this from scratch, incorporating the contrast square, or update an existing cushion with an appliqué panel.

WINDOW SEATS

Make the most of a window seat, if you have one. Here, a short, wide cushion perfectly suits the proportions of a wide windowsill that can double up as a place to perch. Made of dark fabric with large white buttons for contrast, it makes a smart modern statement.

▼ *This made-to-measure window seat cushion invites guests to use the area as a more permanent part of the seating plan – a comfortable place to enjoy the view. The cover is made from traditional linen glass cloths. The crisp blue and white combination echoes the seascape it overlooks, and gives a truly fresh feel to this generously sized cushion.*

the feminine touch

While piping gives cushions (pillows) a city-smart feel, softer edges bring a feminine feel. Frills, fringing and fraying lend a generally prettier feel, especially when teamed with luxurious, light-reflecting fabrics, such as silks, velvets and brocades. These can all be complemented by pastel shades for a light high-key feel, or rich reds and golds for a more seductive look. The easiest cushions to make are those with no piping or frilled edges – but you can nonetheless add a flirtatious touch with ready-made upholstery trims from the fabric stores, such as fringing or tassels, which can be stitched on to ready-made cushions to give them a whole new personality.

INSTANT FRINGES

This simple round cushion in rich brocade was given a quick update with toning upholstery fringing from a fabric store. By choosing a toning shade, the end result is restrained and elegant. For a funkier, younger look, select a contrasting colour, such as aqua in a similar tone to the lilac. To attach fringing, cut it to length, turn in the ends and hem-stitch in place, following the seam line of the cushion.

EASTERN EDGE

Add a silken tassel to each corner of a neat square brocade cushion for an elegant Eastern look that is pretty and smart. The choice of a soft lilac shade for this cushion lends it an individual, fresh modern style that would sit well with purples, blues and aquas.

SILK PAINTING

Create exactly the colours you want by painting pure silk cushion covers. Silk paints come in a wonderful range of colours that can be mixed in the same way as artist's paints for unlimited shades. Painted on to silk, they take on a soft, almost translucent sheen that has a delightful watercolour effect. If you're not confident with the brush, try simple patterns. Draw them on paper first, before transferring them to the silk for painting.

SOFT COLOUR

Use cushions to moderate or update a colour scheme. This powder-blue and white room takes on a new elegance with the addition of smart grey cushions. The plush velvet and cool silk keep the look soft and feminine, but the grey knocks back the potential sugariness of the blue, smartening up the whole interior.

PIPING AND FRILLS

Frilled cushions bring a definite girly feel to the whole interior. Use just one or two to soften an otherwise unembellished room, or scatter them liberally for an undeniably pretty look. Piping used in conjunction with a frilled edging, as here, sharpens up the whole look, lending structure to the cushion. The piped frill around this cushion emphasizes the lovely texture of the silk dupion cover.

style with throws

Throws bring instant change. You can use them to cover up tired old sofas, cosy up in winter time, or brighten up for summer. Since they are easy and relatively inexpensive to change, you can use throws to make an instant fashion statement. If tartan is your Christmas theme, reinforce it with some tartan throws; in summer bring on the bright florals. If faux animal skins are this season's look, just toss one over the back of the sofa. If a particular colour is the current vogue, a throw in that colour will spare the cost of a new suite. If you have a favourite throw, it can be repeatedly adapted with beads, appliqué, trims and edgings to keep your living room constantly updated.

▶ COLOURFUL APPLIQUE

Add colour to plain fabric with bright appliqué. These pots on heavy-duty cream calico are 'planted' with flowers to make a jolly summer throw. The flowers were painted on first so they appeared to grow from the hem. The pots were cut out from stripy fabric, hemmed then sewn on.

▶ NEATLY FOLDED

An elegant throw, which is folded and neatly laid over the arm or back of a chair or sofa, rather than spread out across it, creates an entirely different look.

▶ BEADED THROW

Beading the fringe of a ready-made throw adds interest and colour, as well as extra weight, which helps it to hang better. Brightly painted wooden beads are ideal for fringing a plain cotton throw, as they are lightweight and tend to have large holes. Combine them with an occasional metallic bead to catch the light and give the design definition. Thread the beads on using a short piece of florist's wire. Bend the wire double around a piece of fringe, then thread the bead on to the wire. Pull the wire, and then the piece of fringe, through the bead. Knot the end of the fringe to secure the bead in place.

FELTED ORGANZA THROW

This exquisite translucent throw looks wonderful all year round. Light enough for a summer look, it becomes almost frosty in winter. It is made up in layers to lend a feeling of depth to the finished piece. Natural merino wool fibres are sandwiched between layers of net and organza and then felted together to create a soft, elegant throw.

NEW LOOKS FOR OLD BLANKETS

Dye an old blanket and bind the edges with luxurious wide velvet ribbon and narrow ruffled ribbon edging to give it a new identity.

HANDS AND HEARTS THROW

This all-American throw features a Shaker motif that symbolizes the motto 'Hands to Work and Hearts to God'. The hands were cut out of homespun-style fabric, using a real hand as a template, then stitched on by machine using a fine zigzag stitch.

lamps and shades

Lighting in modern homes no longer has to depend on lamps, since recessed ceiling and floor lights can give us subtle illumination wherever we want it. Nevertheless, we still love lamps for all their romantic connotations and the ambience they bring to a room. Existing light fittings and sconces can be given a quick makeover, while replacing an old lampshade with a customized new one is inexpensive and very easy. It is also worth giving some thought to how your light fittings actually light the room: are there dull corners that need livening up with some light and colour, is your central light far too bright, and do you need to make the lighting scheme more flexible, so that there is something to suit every occasion and mood?

▲ *The square chequered shade of this essentially classic wall sconce gives it an undeniably contemporary feel. Positioned just below a high shelf, it brings the eye level upwards, enhancing the display.*

WALL SCONCES

Wall sconces are usually used to highlight a mirror or picture, but can become a feature themselves. They should be in keeping with the rest of the décor. Position a pair above the fireplace or on either side of a piece of furniture such as a side table. An electrician will have to chase the cables for new lighting into the wall, and obviously this is best done before any large-scale re-decoration takes place. This pretty little classic sconce with a pair of shades and crystal drops makes a feature of a charming painted side table. The gold coachlines on the shades echo the gilded highlights of the table.

▶ *The flamboyant bow decorating this traditional sconce gives it stacks of personality. The lamp is one of a pair set either side of a beautiful antique French gilded mirror, lending it added importance.*

SPARKLING BEADS

Round and teardrop shaped glass beads in harmonizing tones of blue, green and purple make a delicate, sparkling fringe to transform a plain ready-made shade. This traditional trimming looks perfectly at home on a modern lamp and the little beads add a pretty sparkle whether the lamp is on or off.

1 Thread the beads together using a needle and thread and then sew into position on the lower edge of the lampshade. Repeat until the fringe is complete, making sure that you keep the distance between each thread the same.

2 Cut a length of ribbon to fit around the lower edge of the shade, plus 2.5 cm/1 in turning allowance. Apply a line of glue around the shade and press the ribbon in place, concealing all the threads and finishing the lamp off neatly. Turn the ribbon end under and glue it in place.

REFLECTING LIGHTS

The original purpose of chandelier drops, in the days when rooms were lit by candles, was to reflect and magnify the available light. The result was a wonderful show of twinkling lights. A similar effect can be reproduced using various other light-reflective materials, such as glass beads, tiny mirrors, gilded droplets, or even metal nuggets and sequins. These can be used simply as trims, or can be used to form a complete lampshade. Here, tiny glass seed beads have been made up into a delightful candle shade. The beads were first threaded on to florist's wire and then wound round a wire lampshade base from top to bottom. Vertical wires, one at each quarter, keeps the whole shade rigid.

decorated lamps

The three-dimensional, structural quality of lamps gives them a sculptural feel. Indeed, since modern recessed lighting means traditional lamps are no longer needed to simply provide light, we now choose them more for their decorative appeal than for the light they emit. We can also add our own decoration to either lamp or shade, or both, to give them extra appeal or bring them in line with the surrounding décor. Coolie shades, especially, lend themselves to decoration, providing a smooth, conical surface that can be painted, printed, pricked or even given an extra dimension with collage. Depending on what they are made of, lamp bases, too, can be decorated using various media, including paint, paper or even vibrant ceramic tile mosaic work.

▼ NEUTRAL TONES

Classic neutral tones will always look elegant, whatever the colour scheme. There is also a certain logic to choosing neutral lampshades as they won't affect the colour of the light emitted from the bulb. Also, because we know lamps are a source of light, even when they are turned off, it 'feels right' for shades to be of a pale colour, somehow subconciously continuing to represent or reflect light. Elegantly pin-pricked motifs add subtle detail to this plain cream shade, and a pretty sparkle as the light shines through the holes when the lamp is lit. Make tracings of your chosen motif and secure them, evenly spaced, to the inside of the shade. Prick through the shapes using dressmaker's pins to make the holes.

▲ *Add majestic style to a simple parchment shade by lightly dusting on gilt powder, then stamping or stencilling on a heraldic fleur-de-lys design.*

▲ *A wide choice of natural materials can be used to decorate lampshades. Here, dried bay leaves and jute household string, made up into bows and defining the top and bottom rims, make a pleasing combination that has unpretentious charm. An added bonus with using scented natural elements is that when the light is turned on, the wonderful aroma of bay will gradually permeate the room.*

◄ *Chic 70s retro styling, using an all-over design made up of an assortment of ovals has completely transformed this simple wooden lamp base. The motifs were cut from fine wood veneers in coffee and cream shades and stuck to the base using wood glue. The key to recapturing the style of the era was in choosing a smooth-sided lamp base, and placing ovals within ovals, carefully positioning them off-centre.*

INSTANT COLOUR

From a decorative standpoint, coloured lamps have a totally different function to neutral lamps. Instead of trying to emulate natural light, even when turned off, they are there to provide accents to the room. Since lamps and their shades are a small element of the décor, you can afford to use intense colours that accentuate or contrast with the rest of the furnishings. When a lamp is turned on, the colour of the shade will affect the light emitted by the bulb, lending, for example, a red cast to the room. This atmospheric lighting can be planned as part of the colour scheme, but you will need additional functional lighting if you are planning any kind of close work, such as sewing or reading, in the room. While complementing the colour scheme of a room, vibrant hues can also be used to bring an element of humour to shades. This exotic-coloured lampshade in pink, lime, violet and orange cannot fail to raise the spirits. The lampshade, which is defined by a cheery black bobble trim, provides a sharp accent against the softer yellow of the walls.

▼ *Vertical stripes have been drawn on this shade using pastel crayons. They are complemented by horizontal stripes painted on the ceramic base in enamels.*

▼ *The deep purple tones of this small shade imbue the whole lamp with a sense of importance. If used on the walls, the colour would have been overwhelming.*

▼ *Unusually for such a colourful lampshade, this creates the impression of light due to glinting metal sequins mounted on shiny metal-shot organza.*

candles and votives

Go right back to basics and use plenty of candles to bring a special cheer to dark evenings. Flickering golden candlelight creates a uniquely intimate atmosphere in a living room, and, although it is most closely associated with winter festivities, it will conjure up a party spirit at any time of year. Create impact with masses of candles, whether you use groups of tall altar candles or tiny tealights in glittering glass containers.

UNUSUAL HOLDERS

These exquisite antique pieces of porcelain should be used for special occasions and kept on permanent display. For an extra special event but the addition of candles gives them new, magical appeal. There is no reason why other pieces of crockery can't be used for holding candles, use chunky mugs for an informal supper or children's tea party.

DRIFTWOOD CANDLESTICK

This sculptural piece was made by gluing and binding two pieces of wood together, using florist's wire. More wire holds two white feathers, as if floating, for a breathtakingly simple result. Make sure a candlestick of this kind is very stable before you light the candle.

▲ White church candles are the most versatile of all. They always look timeless and elegant, and can be bought in innumerable heights and thicknesses to suit any occasion.

SHELL LAMPS

Oyster shells make charming individual candle holders that are perfect for a temporary display on a low table. Group them together for added effect, and more light, as the transluscent shells softly reflect the flames. Here, pale pink roses add a romantic feel to the display.

SPARKLING GLASS

Fill a pressed glass collection with candles for a sparkling effect. Even the most disparate group, which might include cake stands and jam jars as well as candlesticks, can look lovely, and will provide a flood of light in the room. Arranged near a window on a winter's evening, the beautiful warming glow is a wonderful way to welcome visitors who are arriving after dark.

living sculpture

Use bold, structural houseplants as organic sculptures and to introduce life into living spaces. Since living rooms tend to be warmer, drier and lighter than other parts of the house, they are the ideal place to keep architectural plants. A large specimen plant can bring height to the corner of the room, while low-growing plants can be grouped to form a miniature garden on the coffee table, providing low-key interest that does not interfere with conversation. Before investing in a plant, ensure that it will be happy indoors on a permanent basis. Some, such as bamboo, need to be placed outdoors for a 'holiday' from time to time.

A MINIATURE GARDEN

The wide range of sedum varieties offers a choice of colour and texture that can be arranged in a simple tray. Sprinkle the soil with a mulch of broken shells.

SIZE MATTERS

Modern minimalist interiors look better when accessories are fewer but larger. This giant *Heliconia*, planted in an ivory-coloured stone vase, is dramatic enough to be all you need in a plain white room.

GREAT PLAIN GRASS

A tray of vibrant green sprouted wheat grass (*Elymus*) makes a witty coffee table adornment, bringing life to a minimal living room. White pebbles both disguise the soil and tone with the rest of the décor, while offsetting the grass.

THREE OF A KIND

Beautiful structural plants, such as these graceful *Kalanchoe thyrsiflora*, with their pale green leaves dusted with the finest grey bloom, make a graceful statement in the home. Arranging them in a row of simple terracotta pots emphasizes their architectural function.

floral art

Flowering plants and floral arrangements bring an organic element to an interior, adding colour, form and, very often, perfume. Plants are obviously considerably longer lasting than cut flowers, though you can't expect them to flower indefinitely. When all the blooms are over, move a plant to a little-used room and allow it to rest, just keeping the soil moist. When it begins to show signs of flowering again, step up the watering and return it to the warm. As well as placing plants in single containers, group them together to make an indoor garden.

THOROUGHLY MODERN PRIMROSE

The shy hedgerow primrose may be more reminiscent of a Victorian cottage garden than a modern penthouse apartment, but some of its cultivars, such as this *Primula* Gold-laced Group, for example, have a surprisingly contemporary look when planted in the right container and placed in the right setting. This white ceramic plant holder is perfectly matched with the primulas and tones beautifully with the cushions and books. The effect is made more striking by the lack of any other decorative items to detract from the impact of the plants.

BRIGHTER SPLASH

The daisy-like flowers of these magenta osteospermums take on a certain charm when potted into brightly coloured traditional long tom pots, and make a zany addition to a summer windowsill.

A SQUARE OF ROSES

You can bring a little of the summer indoors by planting up a miniature rose garden. Rather than use a single pot, think in multiples and arrange several containers to form the structure to reflect a classical rose garden layoutl. Here, four low square containers have been set in a grid inspired by formal Italianate gardens, yet their simple square black shape makes this miniature garden unequivocally modern in appearance. Using roses of one type and colour continues the contemporary look, but you could also plant each pot with a different shade or colour as you like.

PILLARS OF FLOWERS

These frothy white spikes 'planted' in black and white pots make a striking show in a modern apartment. They have been inserted in fine sand, which supports the flower spikes, keeping them upright. If the sand is kept damp, the blooms should last well over a week.

PRETTY AND PERFUMED

The ethereal beauty of paper-white *Narcissus papyraceus* works well in any style of home, and its lovely perfume makes it a welcome late winter visitor. The stems often need supporting as they reach up to the light, so push some attractive bare branches into the compost (soil mix). This basket was lined with plastic before being filled with compost and topped with moss. It would make a lovely gift.

INSIDE OUT

This indoor window box makes a bold splash in a conservatory. Busy Lizzies are massed in a smart aluminium trough for a striking display, their pure white flowers set against deep green glossy leaves.

FANCY FOLIAGE

Leaves, carefully chosen for interesting shapes and contrasting colours, can make an eyecatching addition to a floral arrangement. Here, a tall and low vase are combined to great effect.

frame works

Picture frames make great accessories that can be used for much more than simply displaying photographs. The frames themselves provide decorative interest, and, when carefully chosen, they can be used to complement the style of the room. As well as mirrors and pictures, they can be used to frame miniature collages or nature arrangements. Look out for beautiful leaves, flowers and feathers when out walking, as these can be mounted to make wonderful organic pictures. Alternatively, you could use these natural materials to make a frame.

SHINY METAL

The shiny polished steel of this frame is as reflective as the mirror it surrounds, creating an overall cohesive look whilst bringing light to a dark corner. The feather imprints add interest, effectively scattering the reflections and providing a contrast with the mirror's smooth surface.

PRETTY PLASTER

Wide circular frames are the perfect way to offset simple motifs, and, when used in pairs or groups, they can themselves become decorative accessories. Matching pairs can be used for symmetry – side by side or at either end of a mantelpiece or shelf – while complementary frames in different sizes look better in groups.

CLASSIC GILT

Gilt frames with generously rounded moulding are a classic favourite, repeatedly chosen down the years because they complement any painting. The soft gold brings light to the painting without vying with it for attention. For a sharper, more modern look, choose gilt frames with flat-fronted mouldings.

COILED WIRE

A wirework frame makes a feature of the simplest subject. This design is easy to make from galvanized wire using a pair of round-nosed pliers. The coils are attached to a square metal frame using fine wire.

FLOWER POWER

Impudent gerberas echo the simple but flamboyant flower shape of a frame that encircles a tiny mirror.

FRAMED FOLIAGE

Make a feature of natural beauty by pressing a few beautiful leaves and mounting them in simple wooden frames. Whatever plant material you use, make sure it is fully pressed and papery dry before mounting it on backing paper. Team framed leaves with vases of flowers and berries to make a pretty seasonal display.

NATURE'S SILVER DOLLARS

Honesty, or silver dollars, the seed cases of *Lunaria*, can be made into a dainty silvery frame for a mirror. Collect an armful in late summer, when the uninspiring grey medallion seed pods are ripe. Remove the seed cases to reveal the silvery membrane within, then cut the honesty to branched lengths of 18cm/7in. Use florist's tape to bind them to a tape-bound wire circle and attach to a circular mirror.

dining and entertaining

Relaxed, modern living has changed the face of dining over the past few decades. Until recently, most homes had a separate dining room, but nowadays, we're just as likely to have a more open style of living with a dining area linked with, or even part of, a sitting room or kitchen. This puts the focus of dining on to the table itself. Given a change of tablecloth, napkins, lighting and decoration, the same table and chairs can look quite different. Quick and inexpensive to do, this easy flexibility elevates dining areas to the fashion high spot of the home.

atmospheric lighting

Whether you're planning a simple family gathering or a more celebratory occasion, getting together to share food is a time for relaxation and enjoyment, so setting the mood in the dining room is always a priority. One of the best ways to alter mood is with lighting, and in eating areas the key is flexibility. You need to be able to create a bright sunny feel in the morning for breakfast or lunch, and something rather more moody and atmospheric later in the day for an intimate dinner. Several different, separately switched light sources – possibly a central main source and some peripheral 'extras' – will allow any light to be used on its own or in conjunction with others to create a variety of effects. Candlelight casts a soft romantic light that is always flattering.

CHANGING MOODS

The combination of a central chandelier suspended over the dining table and candle sconces around the room offers flexible lighting. Wiring the central light to a separate dimming switch, allows for more variety of lighting schemes. Having the lights on the brightest setting fully illuminates the entire room for an open dining feel. Dimming the central chandelier and lighting the candles focuses the attention directly on to diners for a cosy, more intimate mood.

NATURAL LIGHT

Daylight is the best light source of all, complementing both the food and the diners' complexions. If your dining area has an appealing outlook, especially over a private patio or garden, dispense with heavy curtains and aim to let in as much light as possible. Sheer panels, which barely restrict natural light, offer a little privacy, but if you need heavier drapes for warmth hang them on long poles that reach beyond the sides of the windows to let in as much light as possible.

WALL LIGHTS

Whether fitted with electric bulbs or candles, wall sconces cast pools of light around a room's perimeter, introducing interest to the dining space. They are available in a wide variety of designs to suit any décor. This home-made version was fashioned from galvanized wire, its open coils creating a romantic feel.

LIGHT MOVES

Although they look like electric lamps, these pretty shades hide lighted candles. Candle lamps are ideal for dining rooms as they can be moved around to wherever the light is most needed. For example, they would look delightful on a side table laid for a buffet, providing extra light where the food is being served. For a sit-down meal, a windowsill location would create romantic pools of light around the room.

OLD-WORLD EFFECTS

Lanterns conjure up a warm nostalgic atmosphere reminiscent of days before electric light, and coloured glass creates different effects. You can adjust the ambient light they provide simply by lighting as many or as few as you wish, depending on how many you own.

HIGH LIGHTS

Candelabras give extra height to tall thin candles and always look timelessly elegant. When candelabras are used on side tables, dressers or mantelpieces, they raise the light levels, casting pools of light around the room and adding a sense of romance and mystery.

HOME-MADE SCONCES

Wall sconces for candles can be made to suit your style. Here, two small cake tins – a heart-shaped one for the back and circular one for the base – have been screwed to a six-holed angle bracket.

mantelpieces

The main table is invariably the focus of any dining area, and since it is usually in the centre, it is easy to forget about the rest of the room. But any interest around the walls provides the setting and the ambience, giving the table a context. A fireplace with a mantelpiece, especially, brings an extra architectural dimension to a dining room, and offers the perfect surface for decorative treatments. Candles, a dining tradition, sit well on the shelf and will be beautifully reflected by a mirror when lit. Herbs, flowers and foliage are also appropriate, as any organic material complements the food. There are endless ways these can be imaginatively arranged.

CHILLI TOPIARY

A pair of mophead topiaries constructed from dried chilies and contorted willow stems makes a striking display on a dining room mantelpiece. Each chilli was given a florist's wire 'stalk', which was then inserted into a dry florist's foam ball. This, in turn, was fixed on to the top of two contorted willow branches, the other ends of which were 'planted' in a wooden container filled with dried florist's foam. Silvery reindeer moss was used to decorate the top of the pots.

PURE AND SIMPLE

The simplest decoration can be very effective. This willow wreath, sparingly decorated with bows and little confectionery eggs, is set off by a collection of plain church candles. The overall result is an exquisitely elegant mantelpiece decoration that exudes a sense of peace. Appropriate at springtime or Easter, it would complement any event.

NATURAL SIMPLICITY

The simplest organic displays, which focus on nature's beauty, can be extremely effective. These interestingly shaped young leaves, collected on a country walk in spring, have been preserved for others to enjoy. They were pressed and mounted in wooden frames on attractive handmade paper. A pressed maple leaf, suspended between two layers of glass, makes an appropriate companion.

HOP GARLAND

Hop bines are gloriously wild-looking, with delicate green flowers that seem to dance along their entire length. Reaching up to 7m/23ft, they make an ideal base for an autumn garland. They are easy to find around the beginning of the autumn months in hop-growing areas, although as they travel well you might be able to find them elsewhere by ordering them through a quality florist. In the arrangement shown here, pears, which are harvested at the same time of year, have been gilded to produce a festive appearance. The golden colour of the pears is perfectly complemented by cream candles at either end of the mantelpiece.

▼ AROMATIC GARLAND

The delicious aroma of fresh herbs complements a dining area, stimulating the appetite even before the first course is served. A simple garland such as this, made from sprigs of fresh rosemary bound on to thick seagrass string and alternately hung with artichokes and bunches of bay leaves, would grace any dining room. Herbs are inclined to be small-leaved, so search out the most striking varieties if you want to use them.

MANTEL ARRANGEMENT

Mantelpieces are always a popular place to display traditional floral arrangements, simply because they are usually the focal point of the room. The challenge is to create both a visual and physical balance. Position the flowers carefully in order to prevent them from toppling forward. As you build an arrangement, ensure stability by keeping the weight at the back. If you have enough flowers, create a matching display for the fireplace for an even more extravagantly abundant display.

1 Cut a block of florist's foam to fit a plastic tray, soak it in cold water then place it in the tray. Strap it securely in place using florist's tape. Position the tray in the middle of the mantelshelf before you begin to build the arrangement.

2 Insert twigs and foliage in the florist's foam to establish the height and width of the arrangement. Naturally curving foliage will trail attractively over the front of the mantelshelf. In this arrangement, ruscus, *Euphorbia fulgens* and straight amaranthus have been used.

3 Once you have established the parameters, you can fill in with focal flowers, such as the lovely spray chrysanthemums, alstroemeria and eustoma used here.

decoration on the side

Most dining rooms are equipped with some sort of additional surface – a sideboard or side table – for serving food. As well as being useful for accommodating plates, dishes and other eating paraphernalia, this area is perfect for introducing interest at the room's perimeter, which in turn contributes to the overall decorative effect of the dining room. Traditional choices are floral displays and candles, but designs can be as imaginative as you like. Dried or everlasting arrangements can be useful, too, since they add a permanence to the decorations.

FRUIT AND FLOWERS

On a sideboard, it can be very effective to team a floral decoration with fruit or vegetables that form part of the meal. Here, baby squash accompany a bright spring arrangement combining marigolds and orange-coloured tulips and lilies. A bowl of clementines would have been just as effective, especially if some retained their bright green leaves, which would complement the salal foliage used in the arrangement.

LAVENDER 'TREES'

Aromatic twiggy lavender trees make a delightful long lasting dining-room arrangement, and are very easy to make. Lavender heads are simply pushed into a 5cm/2in dry florist's foam ball, which is then fixed on to branches of contorted willow. Finally, the trees are 'planted' into a florist's foam-filled pot. The tops of the pots are covered with sphagnum moss. The trees look great as pairs, with one placed at either end of the sideboard to provide an eye-catching, permanent decoration for the dining room.

LONG-LASTING EXOTICA

Dramatic *Protea* and *Banksia* blooms from the southern hemisphere are always welcome in northern climes in late winter. For a truly stunning sideboard arrangement, team them with contorted willow in a rusted urn. Even if they are arranged fresh, they will slowly dry out to make a long-lasting display.

GILDED FIG PYRAMID

This almost profligate use of figs makes a gloriously decadent decoration for a festive table. The deep-purple figs were first rubbed with gilding paint, then wired and fixed into a pyramid of dry florist's foam, working in concentric circles from the bottom upwards. Finally, wired ivy leaves were fixed between the figs.

LAVENDER OBELISK

Reminiscent of elegant seventeenth-century style, this magnificent aromatic obelisk makes a long-lasting decoration. It is surprisingly easy to make, especially if you can find a lavender variety with large blooms. However, it could be a costly project, unless you have your own lavender hedge to plunder.

1 Score a circle around a 50cm/20in-high dry florist's foam cone, about 7.5cm/3in up from the base. Shave back a little of the cone below the line so that it fits snugly into a 30cm/12in-diameter container such as this metal urn.

2 Using dressmaker's pins, fix a 2m/2¼ yd length of 5cm/2in-wide wire-edged ribbon to the cone. Start at the bottom, working around to the top, then work back down again to make a trellis pattern. Scrunch the ribbon slightly as you go for a fuller effect and to ensure it fits well into the curves.

3 Position 12 dried poppy seedheads around the cone to create a pleasing effect, placing one at the top. Cut the stalks off 10-12 large bunches of dried lavender to 2.5cm/1in long and fix all around the base of the cone where it meets the urn. Working in rows, gradually fill the spaces between the ribbons.

seating decorations

We ask a lot of dining chairs. They have to look good from all angles – backs as well as fronts, as they are what we see first when we enter the dining room. They have to be comfortable because we may want to relax on them for hours, yet they should not be over-generous as we want to get as many guests as possible around the table. Chairs are also prone to staining from food and spills, so upholstery is something of a liability. There are many ways around these conundrums: you can decorate chair backs to add to their appeal; you can make slip covers that can be whipped off and into the laundry in the event of a mishap; and you can choose chairs whose seats (rather than legs or backs) are their widest dimension. For occasions where something special is required, it may be possible to hire what you need.

GILDED SEATING

Classic gilt chairs always look special, especially when arranged cheek-to-cheek along the length of a table dressed for a special occasion. Not many of us keep these for everyday use, but they can be hired easily if you are putting on a significant celebration.

VERSATILE COVERS

Slip covers can quickly update dining chairs or make a team out of a disparate set. They are also a lifesaver in the event of spills and stains as they can be removed easily for washing. This set of covers features eyelets and bold lacing, which lends a decorative touch to the all-important backs. Making slip covers in pure cotton or linen allows the possibility of dying them in the future to create yet another instant new look.

CELEBRATION TASSELS

A smart piece of cord with a matching tassel tied to the back of each chair creates an elegant, almost military, dressed-for-the-occasion look. Tassels and cord in a range of colours and sizes are sold in the fabric departments of most large stores. Choose generous tassels to make a big statement and create impact as everyone comes into the dining room. If you are making a colour statement with the tassels repeat the decoration in other areas of the room, with temporary tie-backs for curtains and miniature tassels for doorknobs and handles.

PRETTY AND PERFUMED

A herbal posy tied to each chair back looks wonderful and releases a delightful aroma as people brush past, exciting the taste buds even before the meal has got underway. Long-lasting floral herbs such as rosemary or lavender are excellent choices as they also have glorious blooms. Rosemary produces pretty pink or purple blooms in spring, while lavender comes to the fore in summer. The butterfly-like blooms of French lavender (*Lavandula stoechas*) arrive in late spring and stay for summer, while most of the other lavenders flower from mid to late summer.

TREATS ON SEATS

Party favours on seats have treasure-hunt appeal – they are so unexpected and the surprise is only revealed once the chairs are pulled out. They look wonderful when co-ordinated with the tones of the chairs themselves. This pretty example consists of an oval gift box wrapped loosely in gold organza and secured with a textured gold ribbon for maximum impact.

occasional table styling

Since the table is the focal point of the dining room, how you dress it can have a dramatic effect on the décor. One weekend you may be putting on a children's tea party, the next an intimate dinner or family lunch. The key is to equip yourself with an exquisite set of white table linens and china, along with some classic cutlery and glassware. These basics can be adapted with the clever use of coloured napkins, decorations or floral arrangements. Significant events, such as anniversaries or naming ceremonies, especially have a lot to live up to. They deserve a degree of formality that lends importance to the occasion, so classic tableware is always a good choice.

LESS IS MORE

Freshly laundered linen napkins, adorned only by a monogram, plain white plates and unfussy glass are the main ingredients for this elegant setting. Classic blue and white plates and anemones arranged in a row of glasses down the middle of the table provide a little colour. With nothing exotic and nothing exuberant, the end result is undeniably refined.

EDIBLE COLOUR

Fresh summer fruit, such as strawberries, raspberries, peaches and nectarines, bring colour to celebration tables. Natural produce has widespread appeal, evoking endless happy summer days when the air is scented with the aroma of ripe fruit and full of the buzzing of bees. Fruit can provide surprising inspiration for colour schemes. This combination, for example, is taken directly from the dark pinky red of the strawberries teamed with the green of the leaves – a rich mixture that is surprisingly successful.

ROMANTIC SETTINGS

For summer weddings and special anniversaries, roses are a universal theme. They are pleasing to every generation and can be made to work exquisitely with an all-white arrangement. Candelabras, champagne and deliciously scented roses are the perfect combination – wedding tables don't come any more romantic than this. The deep pink of the roses picks out the floral motifs of the best family china, and a delicate scattering of petals all along the table brings a touch of colour to the purest white linen.

◄ *Individual napkins can be prettily trimmed to match the overall theme of a table setting, and any flower, or sprig of greenery can be used as decoration. These napkins are loosely tied with vibrantly-coloured pink ribbon into which an aromatic herb sprig has been tucked. This is a decorative effect that takes just seconds to achieve, so it's perfect for a large party. On hot days, or when the table is set an hour or two before the guests are expected to sit down, it is best to choose a non-wilting woody-stemmed variety such as rosemary or lavender.*

pastel perfection

When watery springtime sunshine filters through the window, the optimism of lengthening days turns our taste from cosy winter shades to pretty pastel tones. Dining areas can be transformed quickly with an inspired change of linen or tableware. For example an aqua tablecloth and matching napkins brings intense colour to the Easter table below, but the effect has been softened by the addition of white china and basketware. For the children's tea party opposite, the table has been dressed with pale lilac linen with splashes of colour provided by an eye-catching array of tinted glassware, confectionery, straws and toys.

SEASONAL MOTIFS

Eggs at Easter time have an enduring decorative appeal, especially when they are coloured or decorated. Here, icing-decorated eggs have been tied to pussy willow twigs with pretty gingham bows in fresh spring colours. Confectionery eggs decorate the cakestand and dyed eggshells make charming seasonal containers for tiny flowering plants. If you can only find brown hens' eggs but prefer a paler look, paint them first with emulsion (latex) paint and allow to dry. Then paint on your chosen colour or design in acrylic craft paint. Natural decorations, such as new shoots, flowers and feathers, teamed with spring colours, guarantee a fresh look as the days begin to lengthen.

▶ *Tiny mauve campanulas are planted in painted empty eggshells. Standing in simple white china egg cups, they make a delicate display. Try this with any tiny flowers; miniature violas, violets or a few grape hyacinths* (Muscari), *would make a delightful alternative.*

A FANTASY TABLE

Toys and candies in marshmallow shades inspired this fairytale setting for a children's party. An allsort-topped cake, garlands of sweets, glass candy jars, colourful straws, streamers and pretty plastic picnicware bring a magical *Charlie and the Chocolate Factory* quality to the table and are set off by a plain lilac-coloured cloth and paper plates. By using the food and treats as the theme, there's no waste at the end of the party. The sweets, novelties and decorative toys can be piled into goodie bags to take home.

▶ *These prettily wrapped sweets have been strung together using medium-gauge florist's wire to make colourful garlands that can be used to decorate tables and dressers. The children will love them, especially when they discover they can simply undo the wrappers to eat the sweets at teatime.*

romantic mood

Creating a romantic ambience essentially means paying attention to all the senses. You can put together a light, heady look by using lots of glass, which is a delight to the eye, then perfume the air with richly scented flowers or fragrant candles to complement the aroma of culinary delicacies that will be served. Translucent materials, such as coloured glass, cloths made of crisp organdie or light-reflective metal-shot organza add a feminine but not necessarily frilly touch. Finally, add romantic motifs, such as hearts, cupids and roses. These are all easy to find in the shops, or you can make your own for a truly personal touch.

DELIGHT ALL THE SENSES
Set a table themed for the occasion. For this Valentine's lunch table laid for two, for example, the heady scent of roses and stephanotis, tucked into pink and white centrepieces, perfumes the air, while lots of lustrous glass tableware sparkles cheerily. The soft shades of the glass, cutlery and home-made meringues create a subtle romantic look while little cream cheeses and chocolates shaped like hearts underline the romantic theme.

▶ *Mouthwatering chocolate hearts form a pretty, romantic gift or after-dinner nibble and are easy to make. Melt white chocolate slowly in a bowl set over a pan of boiling water, stirring continuously. Once melted, remove from heat. Line a baking tin with aluminium foil and place the metal cutters on the foil. Using a metal spoon, drop the melted chocolate into the cutters. Decorate with gold or silver balls and leave to set. Wrap heart and cutter in glassine paper and tie with fine linen string.*

WHITE FOR PURE STYLE

A white table setting is universally elegant, but since few of us have enough white china to cater for a really large event, the basic tableware is likely to be hired for such an occasion. If you have the time, therefore, concentrate on detail to personalize each place setting. Decorate plain glasses with egg white and caster (superfine) sugar frosting, tie a flower around each napkin and strew the table with silver or gold dragees. Add a romantic bow theme by tying cutlery, wine glass stems and party favours with light-reflective satin ribbon. For a wedding, highlight the bride and groom's place cards by propping them against an appropriate ornament.

▲ *The elegant lines of clean white orchid heads make for pretty yet smart napkin ties – the perfect romantic complement to pure white linen.*

▲ *Give glasses a frosted effect. Paint a heart on a glass using beaten egg white and sprinkle on caster sugar; frost the rims by dipping in egg white then caster sugar.*

a seasonal touch

Few of us have the resources to change all our tableware and linens with the seasons and latest fashion, let alone bring out different sets to cater for each celebration. The solution is to alter the dining look with readily available accessories. These could be natural organic materials, such as flowers, fruits and vegetables that are seasonally plentiful, or they could be confectionery, wrappings or decorations, which can provide plenty of inexpensive colour or glitter for a special occasion. Use these devices imaginatively to lend your regular tableware a fresh look that accommodates both the occasion and current interior design trends.

COLOUR CUES FROM OUTDOORS

The natural shades of fruit, flowers and vegetables always seem to look right for the time of year they are in season, chiming with the quality of the light as the year progresses. In autumn, for instance, the orange and green shades of pumpkins and squashes can be used as inspiration for harvest celebrations and Thanksgiving tables. In this setting, green and apricot pumpkins and forest-green squash with peachy insides harmonize with the green and purple of the room's décor.

◄ *The combination of purple-pink and green appears repeatedly in late summer and early autumn, so this is a good time of year to use it for subtly coloured table decorations. Here, the tones of purple-veined cabbage leaves echo those of artichoke segments used as a candle wrap. Arrange the leaves of an ornamental cabbage, available from florists, on a small dinner plate. Surround a thick church pillar candle with segments pulled from the outside of an artichoke. Tie them in position with raffia and trim. Set the candle in the centre of the leaves.*

A NEW LOOK FOR CHRISTMAS BAUBLES

You can refresh traditional Christmas decorations by teaming them with different colours each year. Gold and red glass balls are a classic favourite, but they can take on a very different look at each annual outing. Here, they've been combined with orange and apricot shades for a far from traditional, upbeat style. It's a look that can be reproduced at very little cost. Simply invest in a few inexpensive tangerine and peach cotton napkins, candles and ribbons, then make a stunning centrepiece by filling a tall glass vase with vibrantly coloured kumquats, apricots and clementines. These fruit can be eaten at the end of the meal as dessert nibbles.

▶ *Gift-wrapping adds impact to co-ordinated table settings. These gold-painted white tissue parcels, decorated with gilt ribbon and a sprig of gilded greenery, look highly effective in orange glass bowls and are a lovely way to present guests with a surprise gift.*

pure nostalgia

A fresh, feminine look for table settings has universal appeal that transcends time and generations. The trick is to keep the look simple and avoid the temptation to over-fuss the styling. The easiest way to do this is to start by basing the setting on crisp white tablecloths and napkins, then adding delicate touches of decoration in the form of subtly patterned traditional bone china, touches of embroidery and a few fresh flowers. The look works just as well with woven or geometric fabrics as it does with florals. Decorative china shapes in white or creamware, and fine cutlery, are all you need to follow through the look.

PERSONALIZED LINEN

Couching, a form of embroidery that gives a subtle, almost embossed effect, is a delightful way to personalize table linen. In this example, cotton string is laid on and stiched to an organdie napkin in the form of a motif, but you could use initials instead if you prefer. No special materials are needed except for some fine cotton string and matching sewing thread. A dressmaking pencil is useful for transferring the tracing on to the fabric.

1 Trace a motif on to tracing paper, then tape this on to the fabric. With a dressmaking pencil, trace the motif on to the fabric then remove the paper.

2 Knot the end of a piece of cotton string and lay the string along the traced design. With the needle and ordinary sewing thread take tiny stitches across the string to attach it to the fabric.

3 When you near the end of the motif, make a knot at this end of the string, trim and stitch down neatly.

TRANSLUCENT FABRICS

Crisp organdie, organza and tulle can be used to create a feminine look that is far more stylish than frilly. These fabrics lend a lightness to tablecloths and napkins used for lunch and tea tables. They work because they have 'body'. Avoid butter muslin, which hangs limply. For an extra personal touch you can couch a simple motif or initial on to the fabric. Gauzy fabrics work particularly well with pretty china and simple seasonal flowers.

TAKE A FRESH LOOK

Look for the lovely in everyday items. Here, inexpensive teatowels, detailed in red, co-ordinate perfectly with red-rimmed French earthenware. They become ample napkins, while a similarly toned dish towel is used as a runner to protect the white tablecloth from spills. The result is a fresh, pretty setting for a family meal, the appeal of which lies in its total lack of pretention. Fabrics woven with geometric designs never date in the same way as some florals can, which is probably why they have been used in traditional textiles the world over for centuries.

◄ *Blue and white is a perennial favourite colour combination, giving a classical clean, fresh look that is universally popular. Readily available, blue and white household linens can be made to work just as well as the red and white versions. This timeless colourway can be endlessly mixed and matched – old with new, checks with stripes, floral designs with modern geometrics, for example. For the most successful combination of non-matching blue and white linens, team at least three different blues together. Two can look like an odd mismatch of slightly green-blues and lavender-blues.*

contrast confidence

While tonal table settings create a sense of harmony, contrast can be used to create drama. The sharper the contrast, the more dramatic the effect, with black and white providing the most extreme example. This is a look that needs a confident approach. Use strong shapes to accentuate the contrasts, choosing to keep either to clean, simple, geometric lines, or to smooth, flowing curves. If you don't own contrasting tableware, you could make a feature of a favourite deep-toned vase, candelabra or casserole by setting it against clean white china and creating a strong theatrical effect. A stunning solution for a special celebration.

GO FOR BOLD

For a confident, modern look, choose strong shapes in white for vases and serving plates, and offset them with extrovert foliage, such as these flamboyant leaves. The dark, glossy leaves typical of tropical foliage often come in wonderful shapes. Many of the flowers, too, such as bird-of-paradise (*Strelitzia*) in bright orange and the huge red blooms of the ginger plant, are equally grandiose. Place just a few blooms in a tall, narrow white vase for a quick and easy, yet dramatic statement.

GOLD ON WHITE

Contrast doesn't have to be as extreme as black and white. Old gold, for example, can be surprisingly dark, and can contrast well with white to make a feature of special possessions or beautiful shapes. A combination of old cream and white china highlighted by touches of gold for contrast, can be visually exquisite. The gold itself need be nothing more than a few candles, strands of twine or even a curvy pear gilded with picture framer's cream gilt, which is simply rubbed on.

SHADOW EFFECTS

Teaming charcoal with white produces a theatrical shadowy effect, which is all the more dramatic if you combine beautiful shapes. The more spare a setting is, the more perfect each element has to be. Free from embellishment and with the stark judgement of contrast, there is no room for rough finishes or blurred outlines. Here, the gracefully curved shapes of the china and glass create contrast when set next to the curves of the pewter dish and jugs. White amaryllis blooms set in one of the jugs form a dramatic floral table centrepiece and are all the more effective for the tonal contrast they cause. Their curves and points echo the flowing lines of the edges of the plates.

► *Pretty little potpourri sachets scent the room during the meal, and make welcome party favours for guests to take home.*

cloths and napkins

The quickest way to transform a dining table is to lay a new tablecloth, instantly adding colour and setting the style. The cloth could be purpose-made, adapted with trimmings or a swiftly hemmed fabric length. When you're looking around for ideas, don't stop at table linens – check out upholstery and dress fabrics, too, and look in markets and ethnic outlets. Asian markets are particularly rich hunting grounds, bursting with colour in silks, cottons, organzas and damasks at remarkably reasonable prices. Or look for elaborate Chinese brocades, batiks and ikats from Indonesia and gloriously bold African weaves.

TRADITIONAL LINEN

Scour granny's attic and local antique markets for wonderful old tablecloths and napkins. The quality of the fabric is unmatched in all but the most expensive modern equivalents. Look for plain or monogrammed pieces as well as woven designs with checks and stripes that will never date. The classic combination of blue and white always looks fresh for informal family lunches and suppers.

SUNNY INSPIRATION

Mediterranean people know how to relax around food. Eating *al fresco* is informal and unfussy, and the enjoyment of the occasion is as much about the lack of fussy table settings as it is about the delicious, freshly prepared food. Take tips from this style by choosing simple, colourful country-style table linen and laying it with pottery to match.

A TOUCH OF APPLIQUE

Prettify plain linens with easy appliquéd motifs. Appliqué is much faster than embroidery, and these little cupids cut out of white net, with pearl bead wingtips, make enchanting details at the corners of a simple organdie cloth.

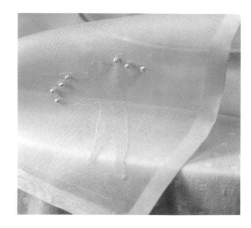

CUSTOMIZED CLOTHS

Tablecloths can provide an opportunity to show off your own creativity. Here, workaday PVC-coated cotton has been transformed by creating a scalloped edge – scallops are easiest to do on a non-fray material as you can simply cut and go. The cloth was then further decorated using a hole punch. The end result is pretty enough to go with the family silver.

GOLD TRIMMING

Gold organza makes an opulent overcloth for special occasions. Trim it with gold furnishing braid and throw it over a turquoise and gold sari for the grandest of parties. You can buy metallic organzas in an endless array of shades from Asian fabric suppliers.

BEADED DETAIL

You can give a simple cotton cloth an exotic edge by using a combination of Indian glass and metal beads to form a 'tasselled' edge. Thread the beads on to a length of button thread and sew firmly to the edge of the tablecloth.

neutrals and earth tones

Inspired by natural materials such as stone, sand, pebbles and wood, neutrals are easy to live with, and when used in dining rooms the result is always elegant. More importantly for dining rooms, neutrals perfectly set off all food types from ripe fruit and fresh vegetables to delicious meat dishes and even delicate desserts. Natural shades mix together happily and can be used to lighten or darken an interior – adding more cream or white for a light effect, or more charcoal or earthy browns for a warmer winter look. A neutral colour scheme also makes the perfect backdrop for a judicious splash of colour, giving you a highly flexible interior.

NATURAL ELEGANCE

Tablecloths and napkins in natural undyed cotton and crisp white linen make a smart team, which can be easily added to or adapted. Using natural fibre fabrics, such as pure cotton and linen, allows you to mix and match old and new, adding more white for a brighter feel, or darker tones for a warmer look.

◄ *Yellow ochre is a natural earth colour that looks fantastic with browns and white. It is an elegant way to bring a brighter hue to a neutral scheme.*

▲ *Natural, undyed materials always look good together. Here, simple wooden beads perfectly complement the warm tones of undyed hessian.*

▼ *Autumn russets and oranges hark back to the earth and are comforting, but they are also high key and invigorating.*

▲ *A combination of rich earth tones without any brightening whites or neutrals instils a sense of security, rooting us in the past when the only dyes were those made using earth and plant pigments. Easy to live with, they can be mixed and matched endlessly without fear of clashing. Use tonal variations and texture to bring interest to the overall scheme.*

◄ *For a brighter scheme, add yellows and turquoise to autumn-leaf russet. The perfect way to exchange warm earthiness for an extrovert summertime feel.*

fresh colour inspirations

Colour offers the most dramatic transformation of any room. This could be a matter of getting out the paint and brushes and giving the walls a new look – but it doesn't have to. You may still be very happy with last year's colours (and who has the time to repaint every year), but you may want to spruce up the room with some new design ideas. You could paint just one wall, or simply invest in a new tablecloth, cushions for occasional chairs, or even napkins. Just a change of table decorations can make a big difference, too, since a new accent colour can cause the main shade to take on a fresh new personality.

MID-BLUES

Blue tones are universally pleasing – just think of traditional china blues, all-American denims and Mediterranean skies. You could use this basic colour theme to ring the changes.

VERSATILE AQUA

Aquas are extremely versatile as they happily combine with so many other colours. They are stunning set against royal blues, and also look good with lilacs, pinks, purples and powder blues, lime greens and even tangerine, giving the potential for many different looks. Add a touch of neutral to aqua teamed with any of these, and the colour scheme will immediately take on an elegant, sophisticated look.

▼ *Adding white to blue reduces its intensity, producing a look that's crisp and smart. Traditional designs the world over combine blue and white, especially in checks and stripes.*

▲ *Lime green and subdued aquamarine make for an elegant, restrained modern look that is nevertheless fresh and light, especially when accompanied by touches of white table linen.*

▼ *Eastern colour sense is far more extrovert than traditional European taste, which is inclined to be restrained, or consist of primaries plus white. This typical purple, gold and pink mix suggests an upbeat celebratory mood.*

LIGHT AND BRIGHT

Red and green may be a classic Christmas combination, but these colours can be used in many more shades than the traditional deep rich tones. Here, the russet-red of a chequered napkin is broken up with cream and set off by the vibrant green of ivy leaves. A bunch of crab apples reinforces the russet part of the theme. Teamed with a pale cream plate set on a pale apricot tablecloth, the result is fresh and lively.

▶ *Go extrovert by pairing hot pink with lime green. It's modern and ultimately feminine, without being frilly. Unexpected colour matches such as this create maximum impact with minimum effort.*

trimmings and edgings

Easy edgings and simple decorative effects can transform plain tablecloths and napkins into something very special. Most can be done by hand and needn't take too long. As well as the obvious embroidery stitches, you can use buttons, beads, fringing, tassels, upholstery trimmings and ribbons to create infinite edging possibilities. Fabric stores provide rich hunting grounds, but you don't have to stop there. Search hardware and stationery stores for string and raffia; walk along the beach to find small shells and explore country lanes, city parks and hedgerows for feathers. Make sure the edging is washable, though, or use trimmings that are easily removed – table linen needs to be immaculately laundered after each use.

EDGED NAPKINS

Whether you are adding permanent or temporary edgings and trims to your table linen, make sure your chosen effect will last as long as you want it to. Seashells look stunning stitched to natural fabrics such as linen, but won't go through the washing machine. If you collect the shells by dismantling products such as wind chimes or shell table mats – you'll have ready-drilled holes for easy stitching. To make these napkins, simply cut linen into 30cm/12in squares and hem. Next make a large knot at one end of a length of doubled pearlized cotton embroidery silk.

Thread it through the hole using a makeshift 'needle threader'. Do this by bending a length of fine wire in half and passing the looped end down through the hole at the top of the shell. Pass the thread through the wire loop and pull the loop back through the hole in the shell, leaving the knotted end inside. Stitch the shell to the napkin edge.

▶ *Clashing colours create impact in sunny climes, but there's no reason why it can't work in cooler places, too. Try a simple cross stitch in fuchsia on orange to create a buzz at your dining table.*

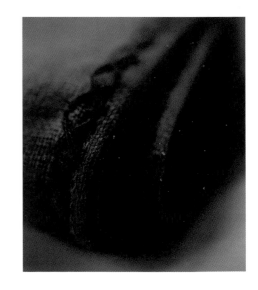

▲ *Borders in matching colours look especially good on napkins when they are of contrasting textures. These shell discs are part of a ready-made trim so they're very quick to apply.*

▲ *Mother-of-pearl buttons threaded on fine cotton household string and sewn on to table linen create a pretty-as-you-please border for a set of napkins.*

▼ *White Ric-rac and grosgrain ribbon, chosen to contrast with the colour of the napkins, combine to make a smart yet simple border design that doesn't take long to do.*

▼ *Old-fashioned blanket stitch takes on a modern feel and looks fresh and bright when boldly sewn in chunky lilac thread on vivid turquoise table linen.*

napkin rings

You can dress up napkins with rings and ties made from almost anything. Depending on whether they are neatly tucked into a silver napkin ring, clasped with a jewel, trimmed with beads or adorned with a seasonal bloom, the same linens can take on quite different personalities. This kind of attention to detail makes your guests feel particularly welcome and the designs will impact on the whole setting when they are repeated on every napkin along the full length of the table.

▲ *Strings of attractive beads wound several times round are charming as napkin rings. To make them easier to use string them on shirring elastic.*

▼ *A neat coil of pistachio-green string finished with a button clasp looks contemporary and undeniably chic.*

ADD A BIT OF SPARKLE

If you use napkin rings with a reflective quality you will add some sparkle to your dinner table. Glass beads work well, and this flower is very easy to fashion. Thread glass embroidery beads on to silvery galvanized wire, then bend each finished length to make a petal shape. Wire several 'petals' together to form a simple flower. To make the main part of the ring, wind slightly thicker-gauge wire round and round the cardboard tube from a roll of kitchen foil or clear film (plastic wrap). Slip it off the roll and you'll have coiled wire that can be used as a spiralling napkin ring to which you can now attach the bead flower.

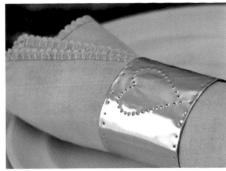

▲ Thin tin can be transformed into smart napkin rings. Cut a strip 15 x 5cm/6 x 2in and wrap it around a packaging tube. Use a pin to pierce holes around the edges and to create a central heart motif. Remove the metal from the tube and fold down the top and bottom edges. Join the napkin ring at the back with silver tape.

▲ Pretty meadow flower napkin rings look delightful on an al fresco summer table. A classic daisy chain is always sweet, while fennel and lavender flowers add scent. Mist with water to keep them fresh.

▶ Make the perfect accessory for a romantic evening by stringing silvery glass beads on to galvanized wire, then bending it into a simple flower shape. Wrap the spare end around the napkin to secure it.

▼ Ranked safety pins bring a smart glint to a modern table. Simply thread shirring elastic through the tops and bottoms of the pins, then knot the ends together.

great ways with glass

Glass is so beautiful in itself that it needs little decoration, but for special celebrations drinking glasses can be dressed for cocktails to make a party start with a swing. There are innumerable ways to adapt them temporarily, such as decorating their stems with ribbons, tassels, beads, feathers or cords. Herbs or flowers (edible, of course) can be frozen in ice cubes, or twirls of lemon or lime rind can be swirled in the glasses themselves. Swizzle sticks and cocktail umbrellas introduce colour. You can also buy decorative drinks coolers to freeze and use instead of ice – look for pink elephants, stars and fruit shapes.

A TOUCH OF GOLD

Fine beading wire – with or without beads – and tiny tassels add a touch of temporary luxury to glassware. For more emphasis, spray masking tape gold and, using a craft knife, cut it into fine strips to fix near the glasses' rims.

▼ *A crowd of glasses on a tray, each holding a gold-embroidered napkin and a gold swizzle stick, is a pretty sight.*

AUTUMNAL GLASSES

A curled dried leaf within each glass provides unusual decoration.

PARTY PIECES

When it comes to medium or large-scale entertaining, most of us are hard-pressed to find enough matching glasses to go around. Self-adhesive 'jewels' and tapes applied to a motley assemblage of glasses will transform them into a beautifully co-ordinated collection.

SWIRLS OF WHITE

You can decorate plain glasses with white acrylic paint, which will easily come off later. For extra sparkle include a few sequins, attached using PVA (white) glue.

presents and favours

Tables set with gifts lend a meal a sense of occasion, making guests feel extra special. It doesn't really matter what the gift is, it's the giving that matters and when it comes to party favours, small is beautiful. A few bonbons, beautifully packaged and placed at each place, a dainty bouquet of flowers, or even a single bloom, all bring a charming touch to the meal. The wrapping itself can be used to add a new emphasis or colour. The same table set with plain white china, for example, would look light and airy with pretty white and pastel parcels, strikingly modern if teamed with sharp orange packages, or wonderfully Christmassy with touches of gold or silver sparkle.

PRETTY PARCELS

Parcels can add shape and colour to a table setting as well as being a delightful element of surprise for your guests. Here, the napkins themselves are used as giftwrap, concealing a box of treats for each person.

1 Place the boxed gift diagonally on a large napkin. Lift two opposite points of the napkin and hold them together.

2 Fold the points down and fold them over again so they lie neatly on top of the box.

3 Fold in the excess napkin on either side of the box and press it flat to form a narrow strip.

4 Now pull the two long corners together and knot over the box to secure. Place each parcel in a noodle or soup bowl.

▼ *Choose colourful party favours or sweetmeats, then package them up in clear plastic and tie with toning ribbons to add special-occasion colour to your regular tableware.*

WRAPPED UP CUTLERY

An unbleached natural linen napkin is used to line a beautifully turned wooden bowl holding horn-handled cutlery. Partly concealing the cutlery, the napkin adds a touch of mystique.

PRETTY POSIES

A sweetly scented Victorian-style posy of African violets laid at each place setting brings spring colour to teatime tables. The posies make delightful gifts that are easy to transport and then simply need to be unwrapped and put straight into a small vase or milk jug once your guests have returned home. No fussing or rearranging is needed.

1 Tie around 15 stems of African violets into a neat bunch using garden twine. Trim the ends of the stalks then mould a small ball of soaked cotton wool around the ends of their stems. Add three or four long-stemmed leaves around them.

2 Spiral-bind the whole bunch – cotton wool and all – with turquoise gauzy ribbon and add a generous bow in purple gauzy ribbon to offset the colour of the flowers.

▲ *Bows are symbolic of gifts, and lend a feeling of giving to the table. Use a wire-edge or metallized bow, co-ordinated with the plate for extra impact to prettily tie up the cutlery for the first course.*

place decorations

Attention to detail always delights guests and adds to the special quality of the occasion. Hosts of larger parties may want to put a name card at each place, making sure everyone has a compatible dining partner. If table space is at a premium, these can always be tied to the backs of the chairs, leaving precious room for the more essential tableware. If you don't want to be too prescriptive about who sits exactly where, places could be marked with a 'lady' or 'gentleman' icon. For example, each man's place could be marked with a rosemary sprig, and each woman's with lavender – and then everyone can choose a dining partner of the opposite sex.

FLORAL MARKERS

Place markers need not be complicated – the most successful are often based on flowers or foliage teamed with a name card. Here, a starched napkin is tightly rolled up to support both the card and some woody-stemmed rosemary, which brings its own aroma and is unlikely to wilt during the course of the meal.

◄ *Hydrangea florets folded into the table linen become delightful natural confetti when everyone shakes out their napkin.*

► *Tie a red rose on to a classic white damask napkin with lilac organza ribbon, to enhance a summer dinner table.*

PLACE NAMES

Chair-back place cards are easy to spot and release space for plates and cutlery on an overcrowded table.

▶ *A pair of delicate porcelain cherubs, along with an elegant place card, mark the guest-of-honour's place.*

GENDER MARKERS

Pressed flowers trapped in resin make delightful markers. You could use different blooms for men's and women's places.

table gardens

Why not bring a little of the garden indoors, using cut flowers, fruit and foliage in abundant amounts for instant seasonal appeal? There are fashionable phases in floral arrangements, but even if you use the same garden blooms and fruits year after year, the table setting can be made to look quite different. Full flower and fruit-packed table top arrangements can look richly renaissance in style, while just a few of the same blooms scattered sparingly over the cloth lends a more modern and romantic feel. For an up-to-date minimalist look, with an architectural feel, go for simple arrangements repeated down the length of the table.

HERBAL SIMPLICITY
Even a simple meal of bread and cheese can be elevated to a lazy Mediterranean-style lunch in the sunshine with the addition of a pot or two of herbs. Here fragrant rosemary and a charming little glossy-leaved lemon tree set the tone for an outdoor repast.

PLANT PLACE MARKERS
Mark each place with a potted plant for special celebrations – a brilliant idea for anyone who's time-poor yet likes to entertain in style. There's no special china, glass or flower arranging to worry about. For an instantly smart setting simply set a line of plants in sleek silver containers as if marching down the centre of the table. Choose elegant flowers like these camellias, and the ambience is set for a memorable evening.

POTTED PLEASURES
Traditional earthenware pots packed with herbs and an abundance of blackberries scattered the length of the table give this setting the ordered feel of an old-fashioned kitchen garden. Yet the sheer repetition of pots and the inclusion of modern garden-pot-shaped soup bowls give this setting a refreshing modern feel. The herbs and blackberries create a glorious colour scheme and give off a wonderfully heady scent, which adds up to an exquisite, if unusual, table setting.

delicious centrepieces

You can make fresh produce the main ingredient for appealing table centrepieces. Wonderful soft summer fruits and exquisite red or russet orchard fruits immediately bring a seasonal quality to the table, filling the room with a delicious aroma and giving the eye a feast before the meal begins. Although most centrepieces are purely decorative, even if they do comprise fresh fruits or vegetables, there are occasions when a beautiful course can double up as a table display. This works especially well if that course is dessert. At other times, although food may make up part of the display, it may not actually be edible – when fruits or vegetables have been coloured or dyed or where seasonal motifs, such as eggs in spring, are decorated for display purposes only.

ORGANIC GROWTH

A centrepiece made of natural elements can also develop as the meal progresses. This one started out as a circlet of sweetly scented lilac and viburnum leaves set in a florist's foam ring. Towards the end of the meal it looks altogether different as it now incorporates the simple but stunning dessert, served in a pedestal bowl and placed amongst the lilac.

WARMING COLOUR

Winter's favourite combination of red and green makes a bold centrepiece. Use florist's wire to secure red apples in an urn filled with florist's foam. Add bunches of crab apples, and finish with sprays of ivy.

A HERBAL ICE BOWL

This incredibly pretty centrepiece is easy to make and can be filled with a no-fuss dessert, such as home-made ice cream. Prepare it at least a day in advance so it has time to freeze hard.

1 Find two freezerproof bowls of the same shape, but which will fit one inside the other leaving a 2cm/³/₄ in gap. Pour cooled boiled water into the larger bowl and freeze to form the ice bowl base.

2 Stand the smaller bowl in the larger one, weight it down and pour cooled boiled water into the gap. Arrange herbs and flowers in the water around the sides, then freeze.

3 To release the ice bowl, stand the bowls in hot water and pour a little hot water into the smaller bowl. Wait 30 seconds, then loosen the large bowl with a knife blade, turn upside down and remove. Turn back the other way and loosen the small bowl. Return the ice bowl to the freezer until you're ready to serve dessert.

GOLDEN ORBS

A little gilding creates a rich, opulent look. Here, a few pears have been rubbed with picture framer's gilt wax to make a spectacular, if inedible, centrepiece arranged on a silver-footed bowl.

DECORATIVE EGGS

Dyed eggs decorated with leaf stencils and set on an attractive cakestand make a bold seasonal table display.

FRUITS AND FLOWERS

Decorating the fruit bowl with seasonal flowers makes for a fail-safe colour match. These hydrangeas started off in vibrant pinks, but fade to fabulous old-rose tones – the perfect match for seasonal figs.

floral displays

By far the most popular centrepieces, flowers and foliage offer endless scope for imaginative arrangements. Make them full and classic for a flamboyant effect, or simply place a single bloom in a glass vase for a knocked-back minimalist style. You can make up one striking central piece or march a row of arrangements down the centre of the table. It's best to avoid anything too large or too high as this could interfere with the social dynamics of guests, who would then have to peer over or through the centrepiece to talk to people on the other side of the table. Alternatively, you can set one stem in a small container at each place setting.

FLOWER POWER
Geometric floral arrangements make a colourful alternative to more usual foliage shapes. Teamed with a rusted urn, these flaming red and yellow parrot tulips take on an architectural quality.

FLORAL TOPIARY
You can use flowers imaginatively to create smart arrangements with an elegant eighteenth-century feel. Very easy to construct, the results are always highly effective and impressive. All you need is an attractive container, a florist's foam ball, a pair of scissors and, of course, plenty of beautiful flowers. This technique does use up a large number of blooms, so make sure you choose flowers that are at the peak of their season and therefore in plentiful supply.

1 Trim the foam to fit the pot or vase you are using, then soak it in water and allow it to drain.

2 Cut the stems of the flowers you are using to within about 2.5cm/1in of the flower head.

3 Place the florist's foam in the pot or vase you are using and make sure it is completely secure.

4 Begin by arranging a line of flowers across the top of the florist's foam. Space the flowers so they have room to open.

5 Continue to place the flowers in lines until all the foam is covered.

► *Mango-coloured calla lilies and ivy make a softer-coloured alternative to traditional red and green for a Christmas arrangement. Add golden glints by rubbing on picture framer's gilt wax.*

▼ *Bring the elegance of an eighteenth-century formal garden to your setting by lining up miniature classical urns filled with Christmas roses (hellebores) in a neat row down the centre of the table.*

▲ *Arranged in a pedestal glass dish, a pyramid based on eucalyptus leaves makes an elegant centrepiece. The foliage gradually dries out producing a completely different effect.*

► *Just two or three tall stems, artfully arranged, can lend a smart minimalist feel to a whole table setting.*

▲ *Even though their design is centuries old, smooth-sided long tom garden pots make remarkably modern-looking containers for mini table topiaries. Make up a trio to march down the table centre, or position one at each place setting. Here, love-in-a-mist (nigella) and scabious flowers are given an extra shot of green with a fringe of bupleurum leaves.*

candlelit tables

The flickering flames of candlelight immediately set a romantic ambience. The dancing flames bring a soft, flattering light that can never be reproduced by artificial means. You can use a single candle to enhance existing lighting, or dispense with electricity altogether and let living flames do all the work. Then the only way to control light levels is with the sheer number of candles. On a dining table, you generally need low or floating candles to avoid dazzling diners as they converse across the table. Hanging chandeliers above the table will provide more diffuse light, while setting candelabras on side tables will bring up general background light levels.

FLICKERING DISPLAYS

Candles combine well with fresh flowers and leaves. This tall arrangement provides extra light for a buffet serving area, where you need plenty of light on the food and don't have to worry about seated guests trying to converse over the candlelight.

◀ *Float a flower candle in a bowl of water and surround it with tiny narcissus heads for a pretty springtime table setting.*

▶ *In summer, flower candles look particularly good teamed with similarly shaped hydrangea florets.*

▲ Thick pillar candles offer plenty of scope for decoration. These have been stencilled with gold motifs and Christmas colours for a romantic festive feel.

▼ Grouped candles can produce a surprising amount of light, and pillar candles offer long burning times. They also look delightful when decorated with dried flowers and leaves.

▲ In a classic combination that is suitable for the most formal of events, tall beeswax candles rise above a perfectly proportioned display of elegant white lilies and pretty purple asters.

▲ Eucalyptus and white Christmas roses (hellebores), set in florist's foam around four candles, make an elegant display. The cool colours are a change from traditional dark green and red.

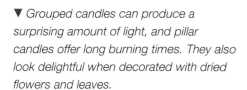

kitchens

Increasingly, kitchens are becoming family rooms. No longer simply somewhere to prepare meals, the larger spaces have become the hub of the household where everyone gathers to relax, entertain friends, do their homework, eat meals. They're informal, unpretentious and hard-working, but since we spend a lot of our time there, we also want them to be as lovely as possible. Plenty of storage space is a priority so we can keep clutter out of sight, leaving room to keep the useful but beautiful items out on show.

colour in the kitchen

The kitchen is the working hub of the home, so it is a room in which you can confidently use bright colours that generate a sense of energy. If wall-to-wall intensity is not your style, restrict yourself to one wall or a single panel. Set against an otherwise calm scheme (or even white), a strong colour will lend impact to the whole room. Kitchen walls, with their many different kinds of surfaces (cupboards, splashbacks, white, coloured or stainless steel electrical appliances), are naturally broken up anyway, so it is easy to introduce areas of contrast that have natural boundaries.

COLOUR SPLASHES

The oranges, reds, yellows and greens of the crockery bring a lively feel to this elegant kitchen, which has limewash walls and creamy-white units. Paint effects such as limewash do require some effort, so it is a good idea to choose a neutral shade that will not date. Accessories in vibrant hues add a fashion element that is considerably easier to change when you feel the need for a new look.

CUSTOMIZED COLOUR

If gingham is your style and you can't find the right colour in wallpaper, try using this quick way to paint it on in your chosen mix-to-order paint. You will need a steady hand and an accurate eye to keep the lines straight, so this technique is not for the faint-hearted.

1 First paint a base coat in white or cream emulsion (latex) paint. Next, prepare a small foam paint roller by wrapping a piece of masking tape around the centre, then, with a craft knife, cut through the foam, using the edges of the masking tape as a guide. Peel off the masking tape with the foam attached to leave a space in the middle. Reassemble the paint roller.

2 Use the roller to paint the vertical stripes. Fill in gaps at the top and bottom of the wall using a small sponge. Leave to dry.

3 Paint the horizontal stripes, using a spirit level to keep them straight. Focus your eyes on a point ahead and your arm will naturally follow in a straight line.

BRIGHT UNDERFOOT

Two tones of orange make up this bright chequered floor which carries a combed paint effect. Although this method of painting and finishing with acrylic floor varnish can be time-consuming, it is a lot less expensive than laying a whole new floor. Simply sand off the varnish, coat with a new colour and re-varnish.

CLEAN SIMPLICITY

Plain matt white always looks good in a kitchen, carrying with it all the implications of clinical cleanliness. Add colour with window treatments and accessories, such as this green set of scales and ladle set off by a smart red window blind.

KITCHEN BLUES

Bring colour and interest to plain white kitchen tiles by using tile paint and different techniques to colour them. Before starting, the tiles have to be carefully masked to cover the grout and ensure a sharp line. It is easiest to do this one tile at a time, sponging or dabbing on the paint with stockinet, an elastic fabric, to create different textures.

PRETTY PINKS

Although pink may not be the most obvious choice for a kitchen, it can be very successful. Warm and friendly, pink rooms lend a sense of well-being. It doesn't have to be over-feminine: pink plaster looks wonderful left unpainted and, teamed with white or grey, can offer a cool modern colour scheme. Pink can also be used with many other colours to create different moods. Here, it is successfully combined with turquoise and green, evoking a wonderful summery feel.

cupboards and dressers

Efficient storage is the key to the smooth running of a kitchen. 'A place for everything and everything in its place, goes the old adage, but it works. If food, utensils, pots and pans cannot only be found quickly, but also washed up and put away quickly, too, the boring chores will be minimized, allowing extra time for rather more creative kitchen tasks. Whether your preference is to have everything on show or hidden behind doors, the trick is to have it where you need it, when you need it. This means not only organizing the cupboards, but thinking carefully how they are arranged within the space. In a well-planned kitchen, the cooking, cleaning and storage areas more or less form a triangle. The major part of kitchen planning is deciding where you want your cupboards. Nowadays, they are more often than not in unit form; in previous centuries, dressers provided most of the storage with cupboards below and open shelves at upper levels. The visual impact of a dresser is still appealing, and many kitchens still incorporate this traditional icon of the heart of the kitchen. How you arrange items on it will have a huge impact on the whole room.

USE COLOUR FOR IMPACT

This dresser houses both functional and decorative kitchenalia and is held together visually by its blue and white colour scheme. The traditional dresser shelves are painted deep blue, and are complemented by a set of modern chunky blue and white checked plates, mugs and a large blue bowl. The overall effect is strong and confident, even though the decorative elements of the display are simply a decoy duck and some sea-worn bottles found on the beach.

MAKE THE FUNCTIONAL BEAUTIFUL

This white-painted free-standing dresser is essentially traditional in design, but fits well in a contemporary kitchen. The white and green crockery, with simple modern lines, is regularly used and far too lovely to hide away. Displayed on the open shelves of the dresser, it adds style and character to the whole kitchen. A regimented row of flowering lavender plants in china bowls completes the display with flair and also adds a welcome touch of colour in an otherwise quite muted setting.

HIGHLIGHT A CUPBOARD

There are many ways to create interest on stand-alone focal cupboards. You can paint them in different colours very quickly for an instant change to your decor. Or you can just decorate the door with a stencilled motif or mosaic design. Stained glass adds colour and sparkle to a plain kitchen. Set in a simple one-door cabinet like this, it plays the part of a painting on the wall, yet provides practical space, too. It gives a lighter effect than a solid cupboard door, without exposing all the contents for the world to see, so they don't have to be kept display-quality tidy.

DETAILS CAN SET STYLE

A traditional dresser, painted in off-white, takes on a very different look when stacked with junk shop finds that have been grouped for impact. Enamelware, antique wirework, metal jelly moulds and canisters, collected over the years, give this kitchen a rustic feel.

CURTAIN OFF CLUTTER

For neat kitchen storage on a small budget you can substitute shelves and curtains for cupboards. Full height shelving and space under the worktop provide storage for all the kitchen needs in this holiday beach hut. Smart ticking curtains, which are quick and easy to put up, hide all the clutter and give the room a nautical look.

shelving

Eye level shelving can lend kitchens a much more open, airy feel than wall cupboards. It all comes down to a matter of style. If you have lovely looking kitchenalia such as casserole dishes, jugs and vases, you will want to enjoy them, so put them on display shelving. Even the most practical possessions can look wonderful if arranged beautifully – and you have the advantage of having utensils to view and conveniently at hand when you want to use them. Or you may prefer to have everything behind doors, dust and grease free. Whatever your style, when it comes to what should be stored where, think in terms of proximity. Keep pans near the cooker; coffee mugs and cups near the kettle; food near the worktops; crockery and cutlery near the eating area.

MAKE THE PRACTICAL PRETTY

A small shelf with hanging pegs both looks delightful and makes useful storage for culinary herbs. Potted parsley and chives provide constant fresh herbs here, but many others can be grown indoors. Fresh garden rosemary, in the wooden basket, and fresh bay leaves, made up into a hanging wreath, both look delightful. They will gradually dry out, providing months' supply of aromatic herbs for cooking. Growing herbs need plenty of light, so position them near a window or under a rooflight and keep them watered. When using them for cooking, pinch out the tops of several shoots rather than cut one or two down to the base, to encourage the plant to grow more bushy.

TRIMMED SHELVING

These shelves have been charmingly decorated with three different trims made from recycled everyday items. A fringe made from bunches of string, knotted over another length of string and pinned in place adorns the top shelf. The bottom shelf sports a colourful fringe of cheap raffia. Like the string fringe, this is made by knotting short lengths in bundles on to a piece long enough to run along the shelf. It can be fixed using double-sided tape, with pins at each end for extra support. On the middle shelf, newspaper bunting, made by cutting zigzags, makes a cheap and cheerful but smart shelf edging.

SHELF TRANSFORMATION

Pretty but practical storage can often be reclaimed from unpromising material. This small wall shelf was found on a builder's scrap heap and given new life with a traditional 'paw print' pattern. The more naive and informal this finish looks, the better the overall effect. All you need is a sponge to give an all over random look.

1 You can simply prime and undercoat an old bare wood unit, although it might benefit from being rubbed down slightly with sandpaper before you begin.

2 Pour some golden ochre acrylic paint on to an old plate and paint the unit using a small decorator's brush. Leave the unit until it is completely dry.

3 Mix some Venetian red with the golden ochre paint to darken it. Dip a small piece of sea sponge into the pain and dab spots randomly all over the shelf. Leave to dry once again.

4 Using a pencil, mark a line all around the top of the shelf unit to create the border. With a lining brush, carefully go over the pencil line with Venetian red paint.

5 When the border paint is completely dry, make a slightly tinted glaze with PVA (white) glue and a brushful of Venetian red paint. Use the glaze to cover the whole unit to finish and leave to dry.

UP THE WALLS

In small kitchens, it makes sense to make as much use as possible of every corner. Here, a plate rack is extended so that every inch of space is utilized, making the best possible use of the space between the worktop and wall cupboard. A trio of cubby-hole drawers make for perfect cutlery storage and below that, wall storage allows plenty of space for soaps and washing up tools.

SHOW OFF

Pretty collections deserve to be shown off permanently – rather than only when they are being used – so they can be enjoyed all the time. These jugs, cups and plates are far too decorative to be hidden behind solid cupboard doors.

kitchen sinks

Now that we have the option of dishwashers to help with much of the drudgery of washing up, kitchen sinks have become a little more lovable, and we can think of them differently. Most of the items that have to be washed up by hand are those that won't fit into the dishwasher – large pots, pans and ovenware – which is why old-fashioned, deep, white Belfast sinks are so practical. Made of sleek, shiny white ceramic, they are very easy on the eye and deserve to be seen rather than hidden behind a fascia. They look particularly good set into a base unit as part of a planned design. Although most other types of sink are inset into a work surface and designed to be hidden from side view, two main exceptions are some shiny modern stainless steel sinks and synthetic white (Corian) sinks. Both these materials can be custom shaped and are made in one piece with an integral draining board for a sleek, modern architectural look.

SINK VIEWS

Traditionally, sinks are usually placed near the kitchen window. The reasons are twofold: first, it is easy to connect the pipework to the drains, and second, a pretty view cheers a dreary chore. Another advantage is that you can grow herbs on the kitchen windowsill, and when you need them, you can pick and wash them in one easy action.

ADD A UTILITY SINK

An extra sink away from food preparation areas is useful for messy jobs, such as watering and potting plants, or cleaning up paint brushes or spills. Even if you don't have the space for a traditional utility room, you may be able to fit a second sink in a corner of the kitchen, preferably near access to the garden.

EDWARDIAN COUNTRY HOUSE

Athough in a moderately sized room, this Edwardian-style wooden sink and rough marble surrounds hark back to the days of vast kitchen empires. The tap is appropriately plain and unfussy, and there is no modern clutter to detract from the simple functional look. The effect is one of combined practicality, and style.

SINK COMBINATIONS

Choose an aluminium sink to suit your lifestyle. Keep it simple with an under-worktop bowl, or give yourself more choice with a sit-on unit that could feature a single draining board or one either side and a range of bowl combinations. This bowl-and-a-half allows for dregs to be drained in the small bowl when the larger one is filled with hot soapy water.

kitchen **windowsills**

The best kitchen window treatments are as free from grease-harbouring frills as possible, and many dispense with curtains altogether, relying on the windowsills to provide interest. The kitchen is the working hub of the house where ornament for its own sake is largely superfluous. Kitchen cupboards are packed with beautiful but practical things such as cups and saucers, glasses, bottles, jugs, vases and casseroles. Take some out and arrange them on the sill, silhouetted against the light, for an original windowsill arrangement. These items can still be used; they don't have to remain 'glued' in position simply because they have taken on a decorative role. Wash them up after use and either return them to the windowsill or replace them with different pieces from the cupboard. This way you can have an ever-changing display.

DECORATIVE FUNCTION

Ordinary kitchen implements can look stunning grouped on a windowsill, especially if they are chosen carefully and grouped with flair. Here, an old metal grater, a modern galvanized bin, glass bottles, an old garden pot and a mortar and pestle make an unlikely but effective combination. They work well together because they are all in proportion with each other and they are all made of natural materials. Don't feel you need to leave this alone, all the items are functional and should be used and moved around.

▶ *Glass always looks good on a windowsill with natural light filtering through it. Collect beautiful pieces, then arrange them in a pleasing display. The deep cobalt blue of this group is particularly striking and unifies some very different pieces.*

SUNNY WINDOWS

Sunlight catchers add sparkle even on dull days. There are all kinds of designs available but you can also buy kits and create your own. If you are starting from scratch you will need to use specialized glass paints. When hanging the sun catcher remember that the glass will be heavy, so you will need a strong wire hanging or a length of fine chain.

CANDLELIT WINDOWS

Pillar candles wrapped in bay leaves and arranged in a metal bowl bring light to the windowsill at dusk, extending a short winter's day. Use thick church candles as they burn down the middle, leaving the outside intact and creating a lovely lantern effect. Thick candles also protect the bay leaves from being set alight, but don't leave it burning unattended.

BOTTLES AND BLOOMS

Make the ordinary special. Here, home-made elderflower cordial has been poured into a beautiful salad oil decanter and teamed with a vase of fresh elderflowers to make an exquisite windowscape. The same idea can be adapted for ordinary shop-bought fruit cordials. Once they have been 're-packaged' in beautiful old bottles, they can be grouped on the windowsill.

WINDOW TILES

These brightly painted tiles add to the Mediterranean style of this kitchen, with its sunshine yellow walls and wrought iron shelving. The tiles are bright and lively, and practical – their impervious surface couldn't be easier to wipe clean.

storage detail

Efficiency relies on detail. The cupboards and shelves may have been decided upon, but even so, the smooth running of a kitchen depends on being able to quickly put your hands on every ingredient, every spice, every small utensil, cloth or cleaner. This means breaking the main storage down into smaller parts: boxes, canisters, jars and containers. Even if buying so many different storage items seem a bit over the top, don't scrimp; they will repay time and again in terms of efficiency and will release you from infuriating rummages through your storecupboards in an attempt to find a particular item. When it comes to detail storage, think in terms of proportion: small jars for small items such as spices, can be arranged within a larger container such as a spice shelf or drawer. Larger items such as pasta, rice, couscous and pulses can be kept in jars or canisters on larder shelves, whilst cutlery can be sorted into boxes in drawers or on shelves.

ORGANIZE INTO BOXES

Boxed items can be stacked on open shelves to save rummaging through drawers and peering into cupboards. If they are not translucent, label them using an icon. These smart metal boxes used for storing cutlery have been marked with real knives and forks, fixed in place using metal-bonding compound. If you don't want to bend good cutlery for this purpose, use junk-shop equivalents or photocopy an out-of-copyright Victorian print and fix it in place.

HANGING STORAGE

Garden sieves linked by chains make excellent vegetable racks and have the added advantage of plenty of air circulation to keep produce fresh for longer. Hung up in a corner, they take up space that would otherwise be unused. As the vegetables are so handily at eye level, they are easy to sort through and select.

HARD-WORKING SHELVES

Double the capacity of shelves by using their undersides as well as their surfaces. Here, jars crammed with a variety of items hang beneath a shelf. First, drill a hole through the centre of each jam jar lid. Then screw each lid to the shelf underside; choose a screw that is no longer than the shelf thickness, so it won't break the surface of the shelf. Fill the jars with light items, such as cookies, candies, preserves, dried herbs or spices, and screw each one back into its top.

ADD CHARM WITH DETAIL

This small painted cabinet with pierced doors originates from north Africa, and adds an individual touch to a modern kitchen. It is used to store jars of preserved peppers and chillies, which add to the colour scheme as their vivid reds, oranges and yellows show through the cut-out star shapes in the blue woodwork.

kitchen **prints**

Highly functional places, kitchens work best when surfaces are wipe-clean, and grease-trapping frills are kept to a minimum. But that doesn't mean a modern kitchen has to verge on the clinical, as pattern can lift any scheme that is in danger of becoming a touch too utilitarian. Designs based on food or utensils are rarely in danger of looking too fussy and work well in the kitchen. Look for appropriately printed fabrics or print your own (it's not as difficult as you may think). Alternatively, you could make a strong contemporary statement by using food or drink packaging for applying decoupage to cupboard doors, drawer fronts, old wooden chairs or accessories. A print-effect design, however it is applied, has a strong graphic quality with automatic relevance to the kitchen, and when you get bored with the design, you can easily update it.

FLOWERY TRAY

Place small flowers or petals between blotting paper and leave under a heavy weight, such as a pile of books, until they are completely dried out. Arrange them on a tray and work out a pattern. Paint the tray, then glue on the flowers and petals. Protect with several coats of varnish.

KITCHEN DECOUPAGE

Make a tray from an orange box, available for free from the greengrocer, then paint and decorate it with decoupage, using old prints or photocopies taken from a book of out-of-copyright images. Paint several coats of varnish on to finish the tray.

PRINT YOUR OWN CURTAINS

This printed design was created using halved fruit as stamps. First, wash and iron some cotton fabric – unbleached calico is ideal – to remove any dressing. Choose an unripe apple and an unripe pear, as these willl be firm and not too juicy. Cut them in half, dip the cut surface into fabric paint, dab on to spare paper to remove the excess, then press on to the fabric. Add outlines or details using a black fabric pen. When fully dry, fix the paint by pressing firmly with a hot iron, following the manufacturer's instructions.

FABRIC TRANSFERS

You can design your own kitchen prints using photocopied images from just about any printed material. The photocopies can then be duplicated on the fabric using a special image transfer cream made by home-dye manufacturers. Paint the cream on the image, then place it face down on the fabric. After a few hours the ink will have been transferred on the material.

DECORATE WITH LABELS

Packaging graphics bring great contemporary colour to kitchen furniture and accessories. Beer labels can be peeled off bottles easily without tearing if they are soaked overnight. Allow them to dry thoroughly on a flat surface, then fix them to a drawer front using wallpaper paste. Varnish with several coats of non-yellowing, matt varnish, available from art or decorating suppliers.

STENCIL PRINTS

Stencils are an easy and effective way of printing your own kitchen textiles. This delightful French-style curtain fabric was stencilled using fabric paint, which was then 'fixed' using a very hot iron, to make the fabric machine washable. The key to successful stencilling is to buy purpose-made, blunt-ended stencil brushes, and to make sure you don't overload the brush with paint. Do this by dabbing the loaded brush on to newspaper to remove excess paint before you stencil. You can buy stencils ready-made or cut your own.

country style

Country kitchens were traditionally the hub of the household. Heated by the cooking range, they were often the only constantly warm room in the house, and so became the main living area as well as the centre for food preparation. It was important therefore that the kitchen was comfortable as well as practical, and most featured a large wooden table that doubled up as a food preparation area and focus for hospitality for a dozen or more people. With a living room element in the kitchen, country style embraced sofas and chairs for relaxation and pretty printed tablecloths and curtains. This relaxed style of living, eating and relaxing has great appeal, and is enjoying a revival with today's busy lifestyles.

CHECK IT OUT

Fresh ginghams are a country favourite. Teamed with white, you can afford to go for bright colours such as pillarbox red for a look that has lasting appeal.

COUNTRY POTATO PRINTS

Flowers, fruits and foliage are country style favourites, and, when printed on pure white, always give a light, fresh look that is easy to live with. This simple four-leaf clover design was potato-printed on to 100 per cent cotton fabric. The result should look hand-printed, so don't worry if the image is patchy colour – it will add energy and life to the pattern.

HOW TO: POTATO PRINT

A traditional printing method that gives charming results. Make sure the potato you use gives you enough surface area for the chosen design.

1 Pin an old blanket to a flat surface using drawing pins (thumb tacks) to provide 'give' when you are printing. Cover the blanket with the white, 100 per cent cotton fabric that you are printing on.

2 Cut through a medium-sized potato, using a sharp kitchen knife, to give a flat surface. Paint a clover motif on to the cut surface, using a fine artist's paintbrush and fabric paint. Then cut carefully around the clover shape, using a craft knife. Cut away the waste potato to a depth of about 6mm/¼in.

3 Using a small gloss paint roller, roll some fabric paint on to the potato, then print on to the fabric. When the fabric is completely printed, cover with a clean cloth and, using a dry iron at the hottest setting, iron each motif for 2 minutes to set the paint.

PATCHWORK MOTIF

A corner of a large kitchen can be made over to non-cooking activities. Here, a patchwork curtain wittily establishes the context for tea and coffee breaks. Patchwork provides an opportunity for combining elements of colour used elsewhere in the kitchen. You could even use up bits of leftover fabric.

SPONGEWARE DESIGN

True country style demands at least a little pattern, but don't despair if florals aren't your style. Spongeware is a country classic, yet its abstract quality has an enduring look that has a remarkably contemporary feel. Generally found on earthenware, spongeware is still being made today in Ireland and England.

TEAM STONEWARE WITH BLUE

For beauty and utility, traditional English stoneware is hard to beat. Its clean off-white tones and simple unembellished shapes look good in any setting and are perfect for the country look. Cool blues have a natural affinity with stoneware, and the two can be combined to make beautiful but unassuming still lifes.

country furniture

Designed and developed over the centuries, country furniture has an honesty born out of practicality. Well-made and robust, it transcends fashion, and well looked-after pieces last generations, improving with age. Polished, waxed or oiled pieces are best kept that way, as wax and oil soak into the wood and are almost impossible to remove. Unsightly stains can be sanded off oiled wood, which can then be re-oiled to restore the finish. Shiny polished furniture builds up a rich patina, and experts generally agree it is a shame to remove this, though shabby pieces can be sanded back to the bare wood. The other strong country look for furniture is paint, and peeling layers testify to a succession of fresh new looks being applied over the years. Some pieces were decorated with motifs, either hand-painted or stencilled on – a style that can be copied, even on newly purchased country-style furniture.

STRING TRANSFORMATION

Battered junk shop finds, like this old kitchen chair, can be given new life by binding them with string. It's a great cover-up if the wood is too damaged to be renovated by wood filler and paint. Use thick jute or garden string, and, starting at the top, carefully bind the back and legs of the chair, pulling the string tight as you go. Re-cover the seat with a piece of hard-wearing plastic, leather or heavy-duty cotton, and the chair will give you many more years' service.

PAINTED CUPBOARDS

Traditional painted Scandinavian furniture was often decorated with colourful motifs. They probably would have been painted on freehand or stencilled, which you could try. If you have access to an overhead projector, however, you could use this easy transfer trick to copy a motif from a book or magazine. Photocopy the illustration and enlarge it to fit a door. Photocopy this on to overhead projector film, then project the image on to the door. Trace over the design with a pencil. Try this only on previously painted or untreated wood that has been primed. Polished or oiled wood rejects paint.

DECORATIVE STAMPING

This ordinary wooden shelf has taken on a delightful country feel since being stamped with a rustic pattern combining giant four-leaved clovers, for good luck, and lots of tiny hearts. A plain painted surface provides the perfect base for stencilling or stamping simple designs. Hearts, flower and leaf shapes are perenially popular country motifs, which can easily be cut from potatoes or lino if you're unable to find a ready-made stamp.

BARSTOOL STYLE

While breakfast bars have become a useful feature of today's kitchens, they didn't exist in the past, and finding high chairs to suit a country look can be difficult. This traditional-style kitchen chair, made with extra long legs to match the height of a breakfast bar, offers the perfect solution.

CHILDREN'S CORNER

Children love to play just where you're working, so why not give them their very own chairs and table in a corner of the kitchen? They can build, draw, paint or whatever while you keep an eye on them. Make the chairs special by painting on eyecatching decorative details, such as your child's name, ladybirds, stars, stripes, hearts or any other simple motifs. Prepare the chairs by sanding them down, priming, then undercoating before you paint.

shaker style

Beautiful, practical and pared-back, Shaker style has enjoyed a revival in recent years. Its appeal is the lack of any extraneous decoration, which accentuates the pure form of exquisite designs. The Shakers, a religious group that flourished in America over the late eighteenth, nineteenth and early twentieth centuries, were concerned only with functional design, and followed the principal of seeing the beauty in utility, and the application of unfussy, balanced lines. Their strict, spartan lifestyles would not suit most of us today, but in recreating the Shaker style, we can team perfect reproductions of chairs, tables and cupboards, with simple decorative details to create a homely look that yet suits a modern lifestyle.

SCENTED KITCHEN

By cleverly combining herbs and spices into everyday items in the kitchen you can use heat to release the aromas of natural perfumes. These oven gloves are stuffed with lavender as well as wadding.

▲ *This cinnamon mat is the epitome of the Shaker maxim of beauty in utility. The long sticks of cinnamon have been tied together with rafia. When a hot plate or pan is placed on top of it the wonderful spicy aroma is released, while the mat prevents the heat from burning your kitchen surfaces. Eventually the mats will scorch, but it is easy to make new ones.*

A LINEN KNIFE ROLL

An old-style pure linen dishtowel can be converted into a useful cloth folder to protect sharp knives and carving sets. Made from pure natural fibre and adorned only by the simple stripe and a couple of utility buttons, the Shakers would have wholeheartedly approved. The folder is fastened simply by winding cord around the two wooden buttons.

▼ *A ticking pocket stuffed with whole cloves makes an aromatic mat for resting hot pots straight from the oven. While the mat protects the work surface, the transferred heat will cause the heady spicy scent to be released.*

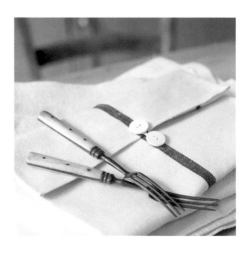

HAVE A HEART

Hearts were an important Shaker motif, often depicted within a hand, signifying the motto 'hearts to God and hands to work'. As universal icons symbolizing love in all its forms, they are a perfect decorative detail for kitchens – the heart of the home. The cranberries on this pretty heart-shaped decoration will retain their shiny brightness for several weeks, then their colour will deepen as they slowly dry out.

1 Thread fresh cranberries on to two 50cm/20in lengths of florist's wire and make a hook at each end of each wire.

2 Fasten the hooks together to make two circles, then bend them into heart shapes without squashing the berries. Lay one heart on top of the other and bind the two together with natural raffia. Use another length of raffia to make a loop and tie to the dip of the heart to form a hanging.

▲ *Introduce gold into the kitchen with a delightful heart made from yarrow (Achillea millefolium). The golden tones, which grace the garden all summer, are hardly dimmed by the drying process. Much of the drying happens naturally before the plants are harvested; all you have to do is hang them upside down in bunches in a dry, airy room for a few days to make sure they are really dried out before use.*

BLIND SIMPLICITY

Sheer undyed linen, turned into a blind, prevents this window from being overlooked. Although typical Shaker style would use homespun checked cotton fabric, the simplicity of this blind pays homage to their design principles.

decorative food

In the country, the boundaries between outdoors and indoors are often blurred. Abundant seasonal fruit, vegetables, herbs and flowers growing in the garden and in nearby hedgerows were brought in both for immediate use and for preservation in a quest to make it last through the winter. Beautifully bottled or dried in bunches and hung up, this bounty of nature would often contribute to the decorative element of a traditional country kitchen, and its appeal has not been diminished by the invention of home freezers, or with the passing of time. The most effective way to create the country kitchen look is to emulate these colourful details. Cram shelves with home-made jams, bottled fruits and herbal oils, and create simple arrangements of seasonal branches, leaves or flowers in country-style jugs and vases.

HERBAL HANGING

A culinary herb hanging makes a lush, aromatic kitchen decoration, perfect for a special summer celebration. This hanging has a well-soaked florist's foam base, held together with chickenwire, so the bunched herbs can be fixed into the wet base to keep them fresh for a few days. The garden pots lend structure to the hanging, while dried chillies bring colour. Once past their best, the bunches of herbs can be taken off and hung up to dry, then stored in decorative containers, ready for consumption over winter.

STORING HERBS

Herbs are at their most flavoursome just before they flower around midsummer, so this is the time to harvest and store some to keep for winter. The best herbs for drying are the woody stemmed varieties, such as rosemary, bay and thyme. Cut the herbs mid-morning, bunch them straight away, using lengths of string or raffia, and hang them upside down in an airy room for a few days until they feel almost papery to the touch, then seal them in beautiful glass jars for winter display and use.

DELICIOUS POTS

Growing food, such as soft-leaved herbs, in the kitchen is often very practical. With more substantial plants, like this rhubarb, however, it is a gentle visual pun, especially if they are planted in a kitchen container, such as this sturdy jam-making pan. Rhubarb can be grown indoors in large containers for a short time only, while the shoots are still young and fresh, but it will need to be planted out in the garden before long as it needs plenty of room – rhubarb leaves grow to giant proportions.

▲ *Flavoured oils and vinegars filter light exquisitely – so display them on a windowsill. Tops made of greaseproof (waxed) paper tied on with cotton string finish them off perfectly and turn an assortment of bottles into a stylish group.*

BLUE AND WHITE EGGS

Decorating blown eggs may be regarded as an Easter pursuit, but once done, the eggs make the most delightful kitchen adornment. Eggs have universal appeal, and, especially if you're able to lay your hands on duck or goose eggs, which are much larger than chickens', they make a wonderful surface to decorate. These smart blue and white chequered eggs look fresh and modern, yet are incredibly easy to do, and it is a job that children love to help with. The design is achieved by sticking on small squares of masking tape, which is easier than it sounds. Cut a strip of masking tape, and cut off squares as you need them. Once they are all in place, stipple on stencil paint using a stencil brush. When the masking tape is removed, perfect checks remain.

BEAUTIFUL BOTTLING

Bottled fruits and jellies are intrinsically beautiful, especially when they catch the light. Displayed in a group on a kitchen shelf they make a stunning display, and if several different sizes are used together they look even more spectacular. To enhance jars further, large leaves can be used in place of more traditional fabric pot covers. Tie them on with string, and they will gradually dry out, taking on attractive, soft golden tones.

kitchen plants

There has always been a happy relationship between the kitchen and the garden, because the growing and preparation of food within close proximity signifies the ultimate in freshness. So even if the plants grown in the kitchen aren't all edible, they nonetheless suggest freshness and bring seasonal outdoor colour to the working hub of the household. Flowers amid food imply the tradition of the potager: a kitchen garden or allotment where flowers and fruit, vegetables and herbs grow leaf by petal to mutual benefit. So gather seasonal flowers to put in jugs or vases, and keep edible plants on the windowsill so you can harvest them for the pot whenever you need to.

SUNNY COLOUR

It is difficult to resist having some edible plants in the kitchen. Miniature sunflowers and a tray of salad seedlings suggest an indoor kitchen potager. The ease of snipping the youngest, most succulent mixed salad leaves from the potager and throwing them into a bowl or even straight on to the plate takes some beating. Filled with goodness, this one mimics a typical outdoor allotment that includes a brilliant summer show of vibrant flowers grown for cutting, as well as plenty of tasty produce. Grow cut-and-come-again lettuce varieties so you can just cut what you need.

RUBY BABY

Old terracotta pots filled with baby ruby chard provide a colourful kitchen display. When young, this beautiful salad plant is spectacular on a windowsill. Its red stalks and leaf veins look fabulous against the deep green of the leaves, especially when lit up by a shaft of sunlight. Chard also has an upright growth habit, so as it gets bigger, it takes on the appearance of a perfect bouquet. If it does get a little over-large and you want to bring it under control, just tie up the stalks with raffia for a pretty display, but the best way to keep it under control is to pick it frequently and add it to your salad bowl.

BRIGHT BELLS

Bell peppers, which seem to become impossibly large for the tiny bush, are fun to grow indoors where you can watch them grow and ripen, and they add a lovely splash of colour. They need warmth and humidity and you'll need to mist the flowers daily to encourage them to set.

SINGLE STEM SIMPLICITY

Not many of us have the spare time for elaborate arrangements; least of all in the kitchen, yet flowers definitely brighten up the working day. The answer is to pick just a single stem or bloom and set it in a suitable container. The less self-conscious the arrangement is, the better the overall effect, so just use a jug, pot or bowl that you have to hand. The key is to choose a container that supports the flower without toppling.

▲ It is a shame to waste sunflower heads that have become damaged at the 'neck' when they can be cut off and floated in a co-ordinating china bowl of water.

◄ Feather-light, this snowflake-like cow parsley head looks enchanting when cut short and placed in an antique cut-glass jug. It looks very different to its appearance outdoors, where it grows shoulder high.

▼ Stately, architectural artichokes make a lasting and glorious statement in the kitchen. Fabulous in this green stage, this one will soon open to show off its feathery purple bloom.

decorative ceramics

Brightly painted ceramics have always been a favourite Mediterranean style, the bold patterns reflecting the outgoing, flamboyant nature of the people and their lifestyle. If you love bright colours, but are reluctant to install – and live with for many years – a kitchen in too extrovert a shade, painted ceramics could be the answer. Either buy them, or, if you can't find the colours you're looking for, paint your own. Even bought plain-coloured glazed ceramics can be painted, though the design will need to be fixed with acrylic varnish. Whatever you decide to do, you can turn the display into a kitchen statement. Brightly coloured Mediterranean-style china is extrovert and mixes very happily. So if you can't find or paint a whole matching set, bring lots of different designs together for impact then display them confidently on open shelves.

MATCHING MUGS

Until recently, to have individually designed china in your home usually meant paying a lot of money for hand-painted pieces from well known craftspeople. If you tried to create your own look, the china had to be used for display purposes only, unless you had access to a kiln. With the arrival of specialist china paints, however, everything

has changed: you can now paint on whatever you like and be sure your designs will last. Storage jars and display china, however, will still last a lot longer than everyday pieces, which really are best fired in a kiln. This set of plain-glazed mugs was made more interesting by adding contrasting decoration that matched the original colours. Keep the decoration at

least 3cm/1¼in below the rim for safe drinking. Clean and dry the mugs, then, using a pencil, draw a spiral on a mug freehand. Mix up a contrasting colour, adding white to make it opaque, and paint over the spiral. Before the paint dries, use the eraser tip of a pencil to draw the spiral outwards at intervals. Paint all the mugs in the same way, but in contrasting colours.

This brightly coloured teaset in yellows, purples, greens and pinks, will brighten any tea-time as well as make a glorious dresser display. Teapots make an excellent choice for decorating as they are usually only rinsed after used.

PRETTY PASTA BOWLS

The simple, unassuming shape of pasta bowls makes them a perfect 'canvas' for decoration. Use a simple but heart-warming motif, such as this dove and heart, which is easy to reproduce. The intense Mediterranean blue, set off by the yellow star and red heart, brings vibrant colour to the kitchen. These bowls were hand-painted using ceramic paints. They were then varnished with matt acrylic varnish to protect the paint.

SALT AND PEPPER POTS

If you enjoy painting ceramics let your artistic skills run riot; you can even paint salt and pepper sets, like this funky striped and dotted pair. The good thing about ceramics is that you can pick up plain pieces really easily, and in seconds shops they can be good value, giving you scores of different surfaces to paint.

PAINTED STORAGE

Storage jars don't need regular washing so are good subjects to paint. Their size and the fact they usually come in sets means they bring plenty of colour and impact to the kitchen. The glorious aquamarine background painted on to these jars perfectly offsets the reds and oranges of the fruits and vegetables.

pretty and practical

Working rooms, such as kitchens, are, by necessity, filled with many practical items, but thiis doesn't mean that they can't also be decorative. Even the most prosaic items can have an intrinsic beauty if they're well designed. Racks, shelves and containers are all essentially utilitarian, yet they are there to gather together various items, and can become a unifying element. Wonderful see-through containers, such as the wire ones shown here, have their own inherent beauty, and they can also show off lovely contents. The silvery colour of wire also gives a slight shimmer to your walls, while the see-through quality gives a small room lightness and a feeling of space.

WALL HANGING STORAGE

Scissors, sticky tape, pens, pencils and various other essential small but unrelated paraphernalia, are often homeless and have a habit of migrating. They need to be kept under control and in a place where they can be located easily when the need for them arises. A versatile wire hanging shelf like this ensures everything is on view, yet kept very delightfully in its place. There is plenty of room for a small plant too.

WIREWORK PANEL

Items made with wire have a lightness and airiness that is both unobtrusive and yet almost fairytale-like in quality, and look good in both traditional and modern kitchens. Showing off attractive kitchen cupboard contents such as mugs, jugs and canisters behind chicken wire could be the perfect solution for an old junk-shop find cupboard with a severely damaged door. The resulting rustic look is quick and inexpensive to achieve. Simply take out the broken panel, then sand down and repaint the whole cupboard to refurbish. Fix galvanized chicken wire, using a hammer and galvanized staples to the original door frame. It won't protect the contents from airborne kitchen oil and grease, but it will stop small prying hands from reaching for your breakables.

WIREWORK UTENSILS

These antique whisks and baskets are typical examples of items produced at the turn of the twentieth century. They suggest the light and elegant refinement of the time, when even kitchen utensils managed to look like graceful dancers. With the turn of the new century, wirework has become popular once again, and there are now plenty of modern wirework designs available to buy. Beautiful utensils like these deserve to be permanently on show, hung on slender steel hooks, while pretty wire baskets make even simple contents, such as eggs, fruits or even piles of crisply laundered dishtowels, look wonderful.

FILIGREE WIRE RACK

You can't get more prosaic than washing up brushes, yet when given a home in a beautiful wire rack, they take on a grace all of their own. This keeps everything in its place and ready to hand.

BASKET OF WIRE

Wirework baskets make charming containers to carry freshly gathered fruit and vegetables from garden to kitchen, as any soil can fall through the mesh. Made of rust-proof galvanized chicken wire, this one keep its ethereal beauty for years.

bedrooms

The most intimate room of the house, our bedroom is an inner sanctum, a place where visitors are least likely to enter. It is where we are most relaxed, where we feel safe and have a sense of wellbeing. It is also the place where our style can reflect our past as well as our present, where a sentimental heirloom may sit cheek by jowl with the latest accessory. Bedrooms are sensual too, natural scents used to fragrance sheets, cupboards and drawers contribute as much to the ambience as does the interior design.

beautiful bedroom walls

The most personal room of all, your bedroom has to please nobody but you. You can make it as pretty as you like, and if the patterns you choose are not to all tastes, what does that matter? The bedroom is the one room where they can stay. It is where you relax and don't have to concentrate too hard, so the lighting, which is most likely to be low or indirect, will enhance any pattern you use. Apply wallpaper throughout, or simply add borders at picture rail level, around windows and doors. Alternatively, add pattern with paint: stipple or rag roll all over, use masking tape to create striped designs, or use stencils or blocks for motifs just where you want them.

2 Hang a short length of plumbline from one of the marks and mark where it rests. Repeat for each mark along the wall.

3 Starting in the centre of the wall, fix strips of masking tape either side of two marked rows of dots to give a 15cm/6in wide strip. Repeat around the room so that you have alternate stripes exposed, ready for painting.

4 Dilute some lilac emulsion (latex) paint with about 25 per cent water and 25 per cent acrylic scumble. Brush on to a section of the first stripe. Complete each stripe in two or three stages, blending the joins to get an even result.

5 Dab the wet paint lightly with a stockinet cloth to smooth out the brush marks. When all the stripes are complete, carefully peel away the strips of masking tape and leave the paint to dry.

6 Cut some cardboard into a triangle with a 15cm/6in base and measuring 10cm/4in from the base to the tip. Use this as a template to mark the centre of each stripe, at the top.

7 Working on one stripe at a time, place strips of masking tape between the top corners of the stripe and the marked dot to create a downwards-pointing triangle. Fill in the triangle with the lilac paint mix. Allow to dry. Repeat for every stripe, white ones as well as lilac ones, so that you have a row across the top of the wall.

8 Dilute some lilac paint with about 20 parts water. Brush over the wall in all directions to give a hint of colour to the white stripes.

COUNTRY MODERN

Lavender and white stripes painted on the wall give this pine-furnished country bedroom a fresh modern look. The broadness and soft colour of the stripes creates an open feel that makes this bedroom even more relaxing. The zigzag frieze just below the cornice adds extra interest, while the striped theme is discreetly echoed in the bed linen.

Painted stripes such as these are not difficult to produce on a wall, as long as you work out the maths correctly first.

1 Paint the walls white. With a pencil, mark the centre of the most important wall, at the top. Make marks 7.5cm/3in either side of this, then every 15cm/6in around the room until the marks meet at the least noticeable corner.

REPEAT PATTERN

Accessories in this romantically decorated bedroom have been carefully selected to match the wallpaper design of floating cherubs and establish a romantic theme. While the figures are only barely suggested in the canopy fabric, they are quite boldly depicted on the occasional cushions, where they playfully cavort with musical instruments. The cream and coffee tones used throughout work superbly well together to create a luxurious and sensual feel that is relieved here and there by the use of pure white linen. Lace borders serve to unify these different items. Freshly cut garden blooms stand in a co-ordinating vase by the bed, where they can release their delicious fragrance into the room.

MIXING PATTERNS

Hand block-printed wallpaper is expensive, so you need to make sure it's right for the room before you buy reams and start hanging. Hang a generous sample in the room to eliminate the guesswork: you will be able to see exactly how the light reacts with the colour of the paper, and how the scale of the pattern relates to the room's proportions. In this scheme, several patterns have been used together, and they work effectively because of their different scales and densities. The walls and two of the cushions have occasional motifs, while the quilt has an all-over pattern. A similar tone of terracotta has been used throughout to create a sense of unity.

clever with colour

Getting the right colour on walls can be tricky because light plays such an important part, and what looks good in one room can be altogether wrong for another. The key is to use colour samples on large pieces of wallpaper lining. Pin these up for about a week, moving them to the other walls from time to time so you can see the effect of the light on the colours at various times of the day and in different parts of the room. If you're using a paint technique that requires layers in different colours, paint samples of the main colour on to several pieces of lining paper. Next, try out various combinations for the subsequent layers, carefully marking on the back of the wallpaper exactly which colour each layer was. Then you will have a record of the sample that works best.

KEEP TO SIMILAR TONES
The walls of this Swedish-inspired bedroom have an all-over mottled wash, with unobtrusive hand-painted white and grey motifs. The subtle effect is easy to live with and, most important of all, relaxing. To

give the design definition, however, tiny ox-blood dots have been added. Being so small, they don't dominate the design. To continue the subtle effect right through the room, the door has been given a similar, but much paler, look to that on the walls.

Dragged in muted tones, it has teaming motifs at the corner of each panel and darker moulding shadows for extra definition. The bedside table has also been painted to match. In a fairly small room, the whole effect is clean and fresh.

REVERSE ORDER

One way to co-ordinate colours in the bedroom is to reverse the background and motif colours. Here, the slate-blue walls lend a fresh feel that is lifted by a stencilled grape border in soft white. The white-painted headboard repeats the stencilled border, but in the same colour as the wall.

TEAM STRIPES WITH MOTIFS

Disciplined stripes ensure that this combination looks pretty but unfussy. Paint the walls in broad stripes, using masking tape to ensure the lines are even. Motifs can be stamped on later when the paint has dried, using a ready-made stamp or one you have cut yourself. Choose colours that give a light effect.

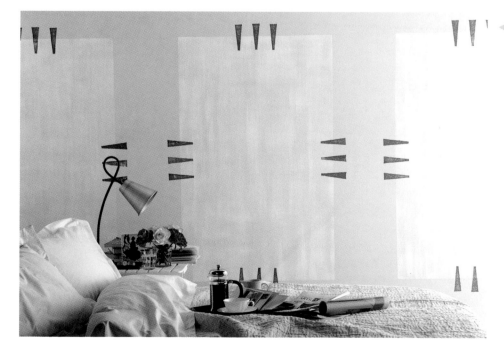

DEVISE A MODERN DESIGN

Choose a neutral palette and abstract motifs to add pattern in a modern setting. Here, blocks of white, washed over cream walls, are given extra definition by the addition of trios of elongated charcoal triangles. When combining patterns on a wall, one trick is to keep larger motifs lighter and smaller motifs much darker so they're not 'lost'. First, paint on two coats of the base colour, then work out the exact size and position for the blocks. Mark up the positions at the top of the wall, then use a long spirit level to get the verticals and horizontals straight, drawing them in along the edge of the spirit level. Mask off the blocks before painting. Allow the paint to dry, then apply the triangle trios, using a stencil cut from stencil paper.

bedroom sheers

Curtains in the bedroom have to work harder than in any other room in the house. Privacy is a must, and in seasons when the sun rises unspeakably early, there's also a great need to block out the light. The best solution is to provide a combination: sheers for privacy throughout the day, with heavier drapes in front or blinds behind them. Soft, light-filtering sheers are always appealing in a bedroom: panels generally give a clean, modern feel, particularly when teamed with smart blinds, while gathered or ruched sheers look good in country-style or traditional houses.

MAKE A NATURE PANEL

Stitched-on pockets to take 'falling' leaves make a delightful nature-inspired sheer panel. These leaves were pressed between sheets of newspaper under a heavy pile of books to ensure they dried flat to be neatly tucked into the pockets. Easily removed each time the curtains are washed, they should last until the following autumn, when they can be replaced with a fresh batch of leaves.

CUSTOMIZE SHEER PANELS

Natural feathers make great trims – they come in surprisingly smart patterns and, free from garish dyes, they go with any colour scheme, be it neutral, pastel or mid-tone. Stitch the downiest feathers you can find to the edges of sheer curtains, matching their tones to the fabric. This keeps the feather firmly in place and also adds a delightful, light-reflecting decorative touch. The smart, striped grey feathers, with their elegant pointed tips, used here, are from teal ducks.

▶ *Feathers are attached to the edge of the fabric by stitching through the quill. A tiny glass bead can be stitched in place on top of each one.*

RIBBON DETAIL

This is an idea that can be adapted with the seasons. In summer, use gauzy organza ribbons trimmed with beads or dried flowers; at Christmas time, tartan ribbons with tiny bauble trimmings would bring a festive feel. The trick is to make single bows that stand neatly to attention at each tab, otherwise the heading could look confused and messy. Also, make the length of the ribbons relate to the height of the curtains. Tall windows can take long ribbons; for smaller, squarer windows, trim the ribbons short. Simple headings like this one also look stunning on simple poles or wires. Even a garden bamboo would suffice as it wouldn't be overstrained by a lightweight sheer.

SHEER LINEN

This hanging panel incorporates delicate pressed wild flowers and foliage for a year-round reminder of summer. If you need to exclude light from a bright and sunny bedroom, however, this might be better displayed as a wall hanging. The heart-shaped leaves are a particularly delightful motif for a bedroom.

FULL OF BODY

When choosing sheers, rather than going for soft fabrics that hang limply, such as muslin (cheesecloth), aim for those with the most body, such as organdie, which is a pure cotton with inherent stiffness.

bedroom tie-backs

Elegantly draped curtains are ultimately feminine and are almost essential to traditional bedroom furnishing. Relying as they do on tie-backs, you can make these necessary accessories into decorative features themselves. Whether you choose formal tailored tie-backs, generously tasselled and richly embellished, or simple ribbon ones, you can use them to stamp your own personality on to the bedroom. Their overall length will depend on the thickness of the curtains – the heavier the fabric and the more interlining you put in, the longer the tie-back will need to be. Make them tone with the drapes, or throw them into contrast, choosing strong colours against cream or white to make a bold statement.

SEASIDE STYLE

Create seaside tie-backs using lengths of fishing net decorated with a variety of shells. Make a small hole in each shell using a drill fitted with a small-gauge bit, then stitch the shells in place using strong beading or button thread.

ROPE IT BACK

Natural rope knotted into curtain tie-backs looks good with fabrics such as cottons and linens. Using your fingers, simply work the rope into simple crochet chains to the length required and then stitch a tassel made from frayed rope to each end.

PRETTY BOW

A simple bow makes a classic tie-back for a lightweight curtain. Here, a wide strip of velvet was folded in half lengthways with right sides together, then stitched and turned through before the ends were turned in and closed with slipstitch. Finally, a neatly tied bow was sewn to the centre.

NET GAIN

Sinamay (hat-maker's netting), is an inexpensive but very useful material that comes in a variety of colours. This green sinamay is decorated with daisies, evoking an English country lawn.

TASSEL TRIMS

A heavy upholstery cord plus a generous tassel makes for an instant and easy, yet striking tie-back style.

SWEET FLOWERS

Garlands of delicate fabric flowers and foliage make graceful tie-backs for a femininely styled bedroom. Co-ordinated with the colour of the walls, they are all the prettier for being set against understated, elegant cream curtains, which gently filter the early morning light.

lighting in the bedroom

As the bedroom isn't a working environment, there's no need for high levels of light, and side lights are the most important source of lighting. Concentrate on lamps that bring restful pools of romantic light to parts of the room, while providing sufficient light for relaxing activities such as reading. The lamps' design also plays an important role in influencing the style of the room.

DECORATED SHADES

Plain-coloured coolie shades are useful if you want to add your own decorative touches as they are readily available and provide an easy surface to work on; they are also available in various sizes and shapes to suit your purpose. Skeleton leaves add elegant decoration to this pale green coolie shade. These delicate leaves were bought from a dried-flower supplier in the early autumn, then gilded at home by rubbing on picture framer's gilt wax.

▶ *This simply decorated neutral lampshade is perfect for a calm white or cream-based bedroom. Pebbles lend natural appeal to the simple card shade, which has been bound with raffia. Look for the neatest, flattest pebbles you can find. The prettiest ones are those that have a seam of contrasting colour running through them, but more importantly they should be more or less the same size. Tie raffia around each pebble tightly, adding a touch of PVA (white) glue under the raffia to ensure the stone doesn't slip out. Then tie the pebbles firmly at intervals around the shade, using the raffia-binding holes.*

SPARKLE AND SHIMMER

It only takes a touch of gold or sparkle to add some shimmer to your calmly lit bedroom. This subtle cream lampshade, decorated with gilded cherub motifs, takes on greater importance when teamed with a gilt cherub statue and an exquisite sunray mirror. When the lamp is turned on, the reflections against the gold will produce a warm, romantic light.

▲ A glass bead lampshade will cast a beautiful, rich light in a bedroom, especially if it is placed in front of a mirror to enhance the sparkling effect. It relies on the same principles as a traditional chandelier, where the crystal droplets were designed to magnify the relatively dim light of candles. For the best effect, use a low-wattage pearlized candle bulb, which won't create any dazzle, and will enhance rather than overpower the glass beads.

◄ Brighten dark winter nights with a romantic fairytale montage of delicate cream Christmas roses (Helleborus niger) and flickering candles, all set in sparkling glass against an old mirror on the mantel. In midwinter, Christmas roses are a special delight, blooming enthusiastically in the garden through snow and ice.

beds and bedding

The bed steals the limelight in a bedroom, affecting the look of the whole room. Fortunately, beds enjoy dressing up, and can take on a whole new character every time you change the linen, depending on the choice of covers. Emphasize wall colours by matching bed linen to them, or change the scheme by using contrasting colours. This works most effectively when the design of the bed is fairly restrained and neutral in colour. A more elaborate bed makes more of a statement in itself, but it can nonetheless take on a limited range of different looks if you pay careful attention to the way you dress it.

▲ TRULY TACTILE

Texture adds visual interest to neutral schemes. It also brings a tactile dimension to any interior, which can be more appealing in the bedroom than in any other room of the house, as we slip between smooth linen sheets or snuggle under a soft furry throw. In this modern-décor bedroom, a throw in nubbly wool and another in fake fur pile set off smooth white sheets and black leather cushions. The result is a strong scheme with plenty of contrast in both tone and texture.

▲ JAPANESE STYLE

A Japanese futon was the inspiration for this pared-back minimalist look, which exudes a sense of peace. A style of bed that translates happily into the modern Western world, it is dressed in simple cream waffle bed linen, adding texture without over-embellishment.

WHITE PURITY

Pure white sets off any strong focal point, and if you have a beautiful bedhead, like this one in elegant antique metal, it is best not to add too much competitive pattern or colour. This scheme sticks to plain white walls, curtains and bed linen for a light, airy, summery feel. The eclectic combination of wooden kitchen chair, metal garden table and exquisite bedhead works well here because the similar proportions and weight of the furniture display a sure sense of style.

STRING STYLE

Team natural string with cream for a relaxing scheme, then ring the changes with pure white bed linen for a fresh look in summer and a soft fur throw for a cosy winter look. Binding battered old furniture with string is an excellent way to bring it new life.

pattern versus plain

When deciding on the decorative style of your bedroom one of the questions you need to ask yourself is whether you prefer a patterned or a plain look. The answer to this might depend on what you have to work with, a tiny or dark bedroom would be easily swamped by a large or varied pattern, but a larger one might carry it well. You may have a beautiful piece of furniture that will, to a certain extent, dictate the style, if so you need to take it into account. Starting from these basic principles will give you a good foundation, and when you have decided whether you want a minimal and plain look, or a more embellished and decorative style, you will be well on your way to creating a bedroom that is the right place for you

START WITH THE BED

When you have an exquisite bed you have no option but to base the scheme around it. This one, made of reclaimed wood and mosaic inserts, is pretty and feminine without being frilly, and the simple country furnishings of the bedroom set it off rather than compete with it. The crisp white sheets are a good choice – adding coloured or patterned bed linen would have simply detracted from the bed's own decorative beauty.

CONCENTRATE ON COLOUR

If you have a bed that makes a strong colour statement, or if you find a fabric you adore, start with that and develop a colour palette around it. For example, this antique bed, upholstered in patterned Chinese celadon green brocade, is a lovely starting point, complemented by plain, pink silk bed linen. The finishing touch is provided by cushions that carry completely contrasting patterns, in colours that marry each element together for a cohesive look.

WHITE STYLE

Pure white always brings a sense of calm and works well within the context of sleek, modern minimalist bedrooms. This style relies upon plenty of storage space: cupboards that visually disappear into the walls, but which eliminates clutter. Tidy away all your clothes, books, lotions and potions behind magical cupboard doors to leave the room clear, peaceful and apparently furnished with little more than a bed and side tables. With everything pared back, white works well as it is not distracting and, being very light reflective, shadows help to accentuate form, accentuating the architecture. Small touches of colour, however, can emphasize the style, whilst offering you the option to make seasonal changes. Fresh plants and flowers are often all you need to bring a touch of colour to a pure white scheme. Choose scented plants, such as these hyacinths, so that they can fragrance your bedroom at the same time.

ADD A THROW

Another way to quickly add colour to a predominantly white bedroom is with fabrics, cushions or throws. This light-reflecting pink throw brings a soft touch to an otherwise quite starkly furnished bedroom.

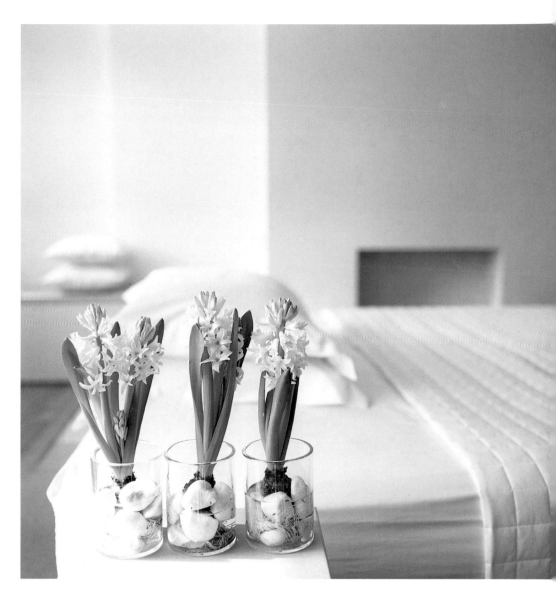

▲ One of the benefits of an all-white room is that it can be quickly adapted to suit your mood. In the same décor a touch of fresh green gives a different feel – yesterday's pink throw is replaced by a soft green one, and a little arrangement of flowers in a matching vase adds the finishing touch.

romantic drapes

Bed drapes are left over from a bygone era when heavy curtains afforded sleepers some protection on chilly winter nights. In tropical climates, mosquito nets were often hung from a canopy, but today most mosquitoes find air-conditioned houses too cold for comfort. However, even if they are no longer essential, canopies and drapes add an extra dimension of romance and privacy to bedrooms, so they are still popular.

▼ BED DRAPE

Contemporary fabric gives a modern twist to a traditional canopy gathered around a top circlet. This is a good solution for those in rented accommodation who may want to introduce extra colour without painting the walls. It would also make a

perfect princess-style bed for a young girl. The hoop for this style of drape can be either attached to the wall or suspended by cord from a hook in the ceiling. The ideal material to use for the hoop is kooboo cane, which is very pliable and can be bent easily into a circular shape.

A colourful sheer fabric is the best choice for the drape, which only requires some fairly straightforward stitching to make up. This can be done by hand, but a sewing machine would make the job much quicker to finish.

1 Press and stitch under a 7.5cm/3in hem along the top edge of each fabric width. Stitch a second row to make a casing deep enough to fit the cane hoop.

2 Cut the cane to the required length, shaping the ends at an acute angle. Thread the cane through the casing. Bend the cane into a circle, overlapping the cut ends. Bind the ends securely together with strong cord or adhesive tape to make a complete circle.

3 At the gap between each width of fabric tie a length of cord. The cords should be long enough to reach the ceiling.

4 Check the length of the drape, then stitch a 5mm/¼in double hem along the bottom edge. If desired, attach a ribbon bow at the front. Tie the cords at the right height and suspend from the ceiling.

THE ROMANTIC PAST

Deep folds of white muslin (cheesecloth) teamed with an elaborate gilded canopy and wall plaque, bring a medieval regal quality to this bedroom, evoking a time of damsels in distress and knights on white chargers. A solid canopy such as this is fairly heavy and should be securely fixed to the wall using screws and plugs. That way, you can ring the changes with heavier drapes. Paler, lighter fabrics can be used for summer, while warmer weaves, such as a tartan or tapestry, make a welcome winter change. Team these with co-ordinating bed linen and fur throws for a new bedroom each season.

STARRY DRAPES

The froth of pure white mosquito netting gives an ultra-feminine look and an intimate feel. Mosquito nets are easy to find in the sheers department of large stores, and are sold complete with bamboo hoop, ready to fix up. The net just ties on, so is easy to remove for washing, or for some simple customizing. Here, the addition of starfish and seahorses gives the mosquito net a mermaid feel, especially as it is offset by sea-blue shutters. Other add-ons could be little appliqué flowers or butterflies, coloured sequins or inexpensive Indian glass beads that sparkle in the light.

modern canopies

The function of modern-style canopies is to add intimacy to the bed in a different way to traditional drapes. Free from frills and fuss, they take on the form of panels, which work well on modern metal four-poster beds and white-painted Swedish style four-posters, both of which are set up to take canopies. If you don't have a bed like this, you could suspend a short length of painted batten or bamboo from the ceiling across the width of the bed and hang the canopy from that. Make the canopy from a simple panel, adding trimmings – upholstery fringing, beads or braid – to the edges.

FOUR-POSTER CANOPY

If your taste runs more to modern than romantic, dress your four-poster with panels for a sleeker look. Since central heating has dispensed with the need for bed canopies to provide warmth, it doesn't matter if the panel doesn't fit the width exactly. Run it down the back of the bed, over the top, and let it overhang just part of the way at the foot. You can edge the whole length in satin ribbon, as here, or add trimmings to the front. Tie the canopy on with ribbons and insert weights in the front two corners to keep it straight.

TENT CANOPY

This architectural style canopy relies more on structure than on draping, and is really a cross between an elaborate bedhead and a canopy, offering just that little extra sense of privacy.

LONG LINE CANOPY

For a bed with a high bedhead and bedstead, a long line canopy offers the perfect solution. Suspend a painted batten on decorative upholstery cord from the ceiling above the bed like a swing. Drape the panel over the batten and hang the ends over the bedhead and bedstead for a cosy tented feel.

bed dressing

The easiest way to make a dramatic change in the bedroom, without going through the upheaval of redecorating, is to change the appearance of the bed. As it dominates the room, whatever you do to the bed will have a huge impact on the look of the interior. The quickest way to do this would be to simply buy your bed a whole new outfit in the form of a new duvet set, or even a new throw. But for a really individual look, you could customize some linens you already have, or make new cushions, pillows and bolsters. Changing the bedhead can also have a dramatic effect, and, depending on the construction of the bed, this can be surprisingly easy and inexpensive to do.

VICTORIAN LACE

Nothing looks more romantic than a bed covered with lace-trimmed white linen. Make layers of scallops and frills on sheets, bolsters, pillows and bed covers. Start by buying a good pure white cotton duvet cover with a scalloped edge, if possible, then use lace edgings cut from used tablecloths and runners rescued from a junk shop or flea market. If you are lucky enough to find one, you could even turn a lacy Victorian teatime tray cloth into an exquisitely feminine bolster. Simply roll up a bolster pad in the cloth, then bunch up each end and secure it with a rubber band. Tie a satin ribbon round each band to completely cover it and to make a beautiful bow.

HEADBOARD MAKEOVER

You can give your padded headboard a face-lift by covering it with recycled curtains. The lining and interlining make perfect padding, so all you have to do is cut the curtain to fit, allowing a margin of 7.5cm/3in for turnings. Smooth the section over the front of the board and fix it in position at the back, using a staple gun. Old chintz curtains are perfect for creating a cottagey effect. The fabric improves with age as the colours fade and mellow, and it looks wonderful when teamed with crisp white bed linen and chintzy handmade quilts and cushions. Use the very best section of the curtain, cutting away worn-out edges or sun-bleached areas. Try to arrange the fabric so that you can make a focal point of an attractive motif by centring it on the headboard.

INDIAN TEMPLE BEDHEAD

Indian temple wall paintings are the inspiration for this arched 'bedhead' that has been painted directly on to the wall. Start by painting the wall in the colour of your choice, then draw out one vertical half of the archway on a large piece of paper (wallpaper lining is good for this), making sure it will fit the width of the bed. Cut it out and hold it in position before chalking it out. Flip the pattern (ensuring perfect symmetry) so you can draw out the other side of the bedhead. Paint in vibrant colours of your choice.

SARI DRAPES

All you have to do to convert colourful silks and saris into glorious drapes for a four-poster bed is add tabs to the tops.

pretty pillows

Sinking back into sumptuous pillows after the stresses and strains of the day is the very essence of what a bedroom should bel about. Traditionally, beds had pillows in plain pillowcases in front of larger, more showy 'Oxfords', which have broader borders trimmed with coloured cording or hemstitch. Perhaps this was done to protect the more expensive, decorated pillows from wear and tear, but nowadays we are more likely to put the plain pillows at the back. and display the pretty, decorated pillows on top of the duvet or throw (rather than hidden under a counterpane). This is a wonderful opportunity to toss some decorative 'extras' into the crowd.

USE COLOUR TO LINK

The red embroidery on this bed cover has been used as inspiration for detailing on three very different white pillowcases. The broderie anglaise-edged pillowcase has simply been threaded with red ribbon. The second pillowcase, with a delicate picot edging, has been given a fine line of running stitches and tiny red crosses on the buttons. Red buttons trim the third. Before attempting any of these designs, check the colour-fastness of the ribbons and embroidery threads by making a few stitches in a piece of white cloth and putting it through your normal wash cycle. The finished look is co-ordinated and delightfully feminine, but most importantly for the bedroom, it looks soft and inviting.

RIBBONS AND BOWS

Simply add bow ties to turn ordinary pillowcases into delightfully decorative ones. Either make the ties in the same fabric as the rest of the pillowcase, or use ribbons to add extra colour and pattern. To make fabric ties, cut them to the correct length, allowing 2.5cm/1in for turnings, but twice the finished width plus 1.25cm/½in. Fold them in half lengthways, right sides together, and stitch. Turn them through, turn in the ends and close with slipstitch. Stitch into position on the pilllowcase.

▼ *Ribbons simply need cutting to length and stitching in position. Choose several in co-ordinated colours but different widths and with different edgings, some chequered and some plain, to make up attractive detailing for the pillow edges. It is a delightful idea for a child's room.*

EMBROIDERED DETAIL

On pure white linen, a few coloured motifs add fresh, pretty detail to an otherwise unembellished scheme. The shape of the pillowcase gives the embroidery the quality of a framed picture, making it a focal point in the bedroom as a whole.

SMART BUTTONS

The contrast panel on this smart linen pillowcase sets off a row of chic buttons. This is an elegant solution for modern minimalist bedrooms in need of added interest as well as those that are a little more cosy in feel.

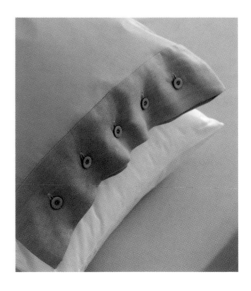

cushion luxury

While the *raison d'être* of pillows is to be slept on, cushions have an altogether different function. Although they are there for comfort, they are smarter than pillows, and give a bedroom its daytime persona. Use them to inject extra colour, texture and style to the bedroom. As well as adorning the bed, they can be used on side chairs, windowseats and any upholstery, transforming the room into much more than simply a place to sleep in. When it comes to styling, it is the detail that counts. Add ribbons, tassels and frills for a feminine look, smart piping, buttons and top stitching for a more tailored appearance. Think, too, about texture, adding sensuous shiny satin and fun fake furs.

GAUZY, HOP-FILLED PILLOW
Hops come into season in late summer. Their aroma is known to be mildly sedative so they are traditionally used to stuff pillows and cushions to induce peaceful sleep. Hops are attractive in themselves, so let them become part of the design by using a gauzy fabric for the top of the cushion. They are surprisingly robust, and will keep their shape.

PILE THEM HIGH
The way cushions are used creates different effects. Piled high on a divan or a bed they generally give a relaxed, luxurious, almost kasbah-like impression, while just one or two are generally smarter and a little more formal.

RIBBON PILLOW
Lengths of different ribbons look quite beautiful when pieced together. This cushion cover, made from a wonderful mix of ribbons has an almost Elizabethan look. If this idea proves too expensive, make the cushion cover in velvet, then stitch on co-ordinating lengths of ribbon, allowing the velvet to show through in several places.

ELEGANT ADDITIONS

Adding a small cushion as a final touch can be as effective as a pile. A rich cherry red heart, set against understated black, white and grey, lends an elegant winter look to the bedroom. Cushions in fabulous tactile fabrics, such as mohair and velvet, feel wonderful against the skin, and a heart shape is universally appealing in the bedroom, even for a modern setting.

▼ *This bolster is covered in a gorgeous, silver pleated silk that looks as if it comes straight from the fashion fabric department. Wrap a full width of the fabric around the bolster and knot the ends. The bolster makes a glamorous swishy addition to quite a formal, almost masculine-looking bed arrangement.*

CUSHION CHIC

Neat and tailored, this cream cushion has the pertness of a Paris spring collection circa 1950. Elegantly piped, it makes a light, pretty accessory for a boudoir chair. Piping always makes a neat edge for any cushion of any shape. When piped in the same fabric as the rest of the cushion it is unobtrusive, while contrasting colours give a more formal look. Upholstery fringing would add a fun Parisian can-can-dancer look. The cushion was given a final flourish with a neatly stencilled gold star. Fastened to the delicate curves of a black wrought iron chair back by means of a little ribbon bow, it is deliberately positioned to give comfort to a weary back.

colour wisdom

The bedroom is where we spend the longest periods of time. It is also our most individual and personal space, so we need to be as comfortable there as possible. Colour is known to influence our moods and even our wellbeing, and therefore should be a prime consideration when we are thinking about how a bedroom should look. Although our response to different colours is affected by our personalities and taste, there are some basic colour rules that we should be aware of. Generally speaking, colours that are restful and calming work best in bedrooms, but we need to bear in mind that as we also wake up in this room, there should be an energizing colour for us to focus on in the morning, perhaps a little way away from the bed.

▲ LAVENDER

Pale purples and soft lavender shades work well in a bedroom because they have a calming effect as well as a gentle energy. Lavender is also a known cure for sleeplessness, so complement your colour scheme with some lavender aromatherapy oil or a bowl of the dried flower heads beside your bed.

▼ *Lavender in soft indigo tones is just the right shade for creating a calming, sleep-inducing ambience. Its wonderful natural perfume, which evokes a feeling of well-being, is an added bonus.*

▲ PALE BLUES

Soft shades of pale blue, violet, purple and indigo are quietening, restful colours that lower the body's levels of activity and help to stabilize natural sleep rhythms. They look wonderful mixed together, are stunning with white, and take on a distinctly feminine look when teamed with pink.

▼ *If you don't have a pale blue bedroom, add a touch of this soothing colour with a candle. Jasmine is said to help clear negative atmospheres, so arrange some around the base.*

ROSE

Pale pinks and soft violets are light and calming. They are also good healing and recuperating colours, so if your bedroom has become a sick room try introducing some pale pink cushions and flowers to aid the healing process. If you have decided to decorate your bedroom in pink, take your time to choose the right shades and try out samples, as they often come out darker than expected.

▼ *As a quick way of adding pink to a room use fresh roses, rose water and essential oil. Rose essential oil is used to help insomnia and headaches.*

RISE AND SHINE

Bright warm colours, such as red, orange and yellow, are good for stimulating the senses. A bedroom that is decorated in these colours might not be restful enough to encourage sleep, but for that early morning energy spurt that is so vital you could try introducing a splash of colour into your bedroom via a moveable object, such as a cushion, rug or throw. A red lamp is perfect, especially for dark mornings, as when it is switched on the light will create a red glow.

◄ *Green is said to offer the energy of change and growth – ideal to start the day with. While it is useful as an occasional splash of colour, a vibrant green such as this would make a dark and possibly oppressive main colour for a bedroom.*

fresh blues

A universal favourite, blue with white is an easy partnership that will never date. It was a favourite for centuries in China, and its popularity rose in eighteenth-century Europe when increased trade with the Far East led to the large-scale importation of porcelain. The legacy is blue and white Dutch Delft tiles and blue and white English Spode china. After all these years the freshness of the combination has not faded and it still manages to look modern. It works with pretty embroidery and frills, yet looks just as good in plains. To achieve a light and airy feel use mainly white with just a touch of blue, but if you prefer a stronger look use plenty of blue with mere touches of white to sharpen the effect. To set it off, just add a touch of pink.

RELAXING BLUES

A touch of mid-blue trimming brings relief to plain white pillowcases and matches a part-blue duvet cover. Within the context of a relaxed seaside holiday home, this bed linen looks fresh and inviting, offering cool sheets after a hot day on the beach. The bedding has been crisply ironed with a squirt of spray starch, adding to the cool effect and irresistible feel.

ANTIQUE BLUE

Classic motifs, reminiscent of restrained eighteenth-century style, add elegance to an all-white bedroom. They work especially well when the metal is painted to resemble the verdigris found on old copper. A vase of fresh blue flowers would introduce a little more blue into the room.

PATCHWORK COMFORT

A hand-stitched quilt gives a cosy country feel, but using large rectangles for patchwork, in a limited colour range of clear blues and white, keeps the quilt from looking fussy or quaint, and allows it to fit into a modern rustic scheme.

DETAILS IN BLUE

One of the joys of blues and white is that they are eminently mixable. In the spectrum, blues stretch right the way from green to indigo, and even if you choose mid-blue, it will veer towards one end or the other. Either keep to one shade of blue and add white, or use at least three different blues plus white. Two blues could be a mismatch; once there are more than two, it looks like a considered plan. Here, blue and white takes on a fresh country feel, with appliqué and embroidery teamed with lilac Michaelmas daisies.

SEASIDE BLUE

Add pretty touches to china blue and white with simple seashore motifs. These shells and starfish have been embroidered on to the pillowcases: blue on white and white on blue.

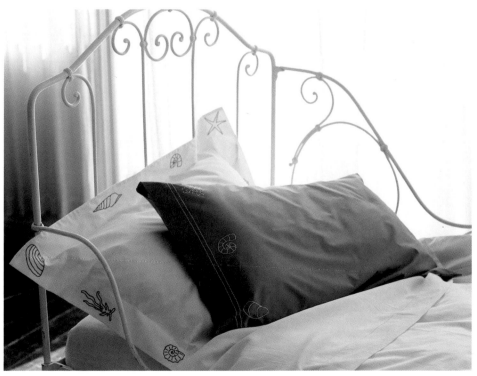

the boudoir

A boudoir is exclusively a woman's place – her sitting room or bedroom. The word was coined in eighteenth-century France (doubtless by a man) to mean literally a woman's sulking room, though even then, the boudoir was seen as a place of rather more coquettish behaviour. It was the room where ladies could indulge their tastes. Sumptuous fabrics such as velvet, lace and silk in pompadour shades, were draped luxuriously at the windows and around the bed. Copious cushions invited relaxation and perfume pervaded the air. A proper boudoir pays no lip service to male tastes. But then, there's the frisson. An invitation into this all-female territory is on a woman's terms, and the male is, quite simply, helpless if he accepts.

▶ SUMPTUOUS SPLENDOUR
Bolsters and cushions in the powdery blue and pink shades associated with Madame de Pompadour, the mistress of Louis XV of France, are ideal boudoir furnishings. Piled on to chaises longues, beds and sofas, they are the perfect invitation to relax. Made of soft velvets and fine silks with tassels and fringing, buttoning and pleating, they are icons of this outrageously extravagant style.

▲ *Ladies in their boudoirs loved their trinkets, and whiled away the hours making everything around them beautiful. This Victorian pincushion, decorated with pretty glass beads, held in position by pins, makes a charming traditional accessory. The pins are arranged in four heart motifs, one at each corner, perfectly fitting for a boudoir.*

▲ *Choose amber brocade to dress the day bed. Rich yet classic and very boudoir, this bolster, with its lavish black tassel and matching piping, makes the perfect transition from a smart daytime look to sultry nights.*

◄ *Figured velvets trimmed with golden cord contribute to the sumptuous boudoir look, while evoking the richness of a Renaissance palace.*

▼ *This collection, comprising the prettiest of heart-shaped cushions in baby pink, a generously fringed 1920s shawl, flowers, perfume, lotions and potions, could not be more feminine. More late Victorian than eighteenth century, this is nonetheless the very essence of a boudoir in its exclusively feminine feel.*

▼ *Reds and golds are classic Victorian boudoir colours, and when the motifs are hearts and cupids, the effect is complete.*

the romantic bedroom

Designed to thrill all the senses, the romantic bedroom is essentially pretty, soft and feminine. The furnishings and bedding are tactile, making use of satins, silks, velvets and furs. The romantic flexible lighting should be complemented by candlelight both for the quality of the light, and because it can be moved around without the bother of trailing wires and light sockets. Ideally, the romantic bedroom has generous drapes, a large squashy sofa with plenty of cushions and pretty painted cabinets, one of which could house a sound system for soft music. There are several things a romantic bedroom does not have – most importantly a telephone (let it ring) and a television. The room is scented naturally by fresh flowers, dried lavender and potpourri.

PAINTED CABINETS

Furniture painted in pastel shades has a light, feminine feel that works well in romantic bedrooms. While a rare find like this cabinet hand-painted with landscapes should never be re-coated, plain ones can quickly be given a new coat of paint to co-ordinate with your room. Matt paint always looks more beautiful, especially if it is put on in layers and the top coat is rubbed back at high-wear areas to reveal the colour underneath.

SILVER AND LACE

Sepia photographs have an intrinsic beauty and look wonderful with silver and lace in romantic bedrooms. You may find some treasures in your own family's archives and attics, but if not, look out for them in antique shops and flea markets.

DECORATED HANGERS

Some clothes, like pretty slips, satin pyjamas or a gorgeous dressing gown, are far too pretty to hide in the cupboard, so show them off instead, hung on beautiful padded satin hangers on a large wall or door hook. These hangers are easy to make, whether you have a sewing machine or not, and can be co-ordinated with the colour of your bedroom or even the clothes themselves. In addition to a wooden coat hanger, you will need some polyester wadding (batting) and a length of wide satin ribbon. Matching ready-made silk flowers and leaves and an embroidered ribbon bow will add a finishing touch to the hangers.

1 Cut a strip of polyester wadding (batting) and wind it around the hanger, securing it with a few stitches. Cut a rectangle of wadding to cover the prepared hanger, then stitch it over the padded hanger neatly, trimming and tucking in the ends.

2 Cut two lengths of wide satin ribbon to make the cover for the hanger. With right sides together, stitch each end in a gentle curve. Stitch along one long edge of the satin cover and then turn it through to the right side.

3 Fit the satin cover over the hanger, with the open edge uppermost. Slipstitch the top edges neatly together, gathering the ends gently and easing in the fullness as you sew.

4 Tie a length of embroidered ribbon around the centre of the hanger to finish in a bow around the hook. Use this as a foundation to attach the flowers and leaves. Add further loops of ribbon to make a pretty arrangement.

SOUVENIR HEART

Make a souvenir heart for your wedding or anniversary, then let it take centre stage in the bedroom for on-going romance. This one has a timeless quality that would look good in any bedroom. The base was made from hay bound on to a galvanized wire base using florist's reel wire. It was then bound with red and gold ribbons, and trimmed with dried flowers.

the serene bedroom

Tranquillity, above all, has to be the priority in the bedroom. Whether yours is a bedroom first and last, or whether it has to accommodate many different activities, at the end of the day it is a place of rest in which you need be able to relax and wind down. Create a feeling of serenity by using soft harmonizing shades found at the cooler end of the colour spectrum, as these are generally more peaceful than energizing strong reds and yellows. Avoid harsh contrasts, which are invigorating, and so unlikely to induce relaxation. Simple uncluttered rooms generally promote a sense of well-being. One or two attractive pieces of furniture is all you need, plus plenty of cupboard space so clothes, shoes and general bedroom paraphernalia can be hidden away, leaving surfaces free for displaying only the most beautiful accessories. Window treatments, too, need to be simple. Exquisite panels, clipped on to curtain wires or tab-topped on poles, offer an elegant modern look, whilst a serene country or traditional feel can be achieved with unpretentious gathered headings that are free of distracting frills and flounces.

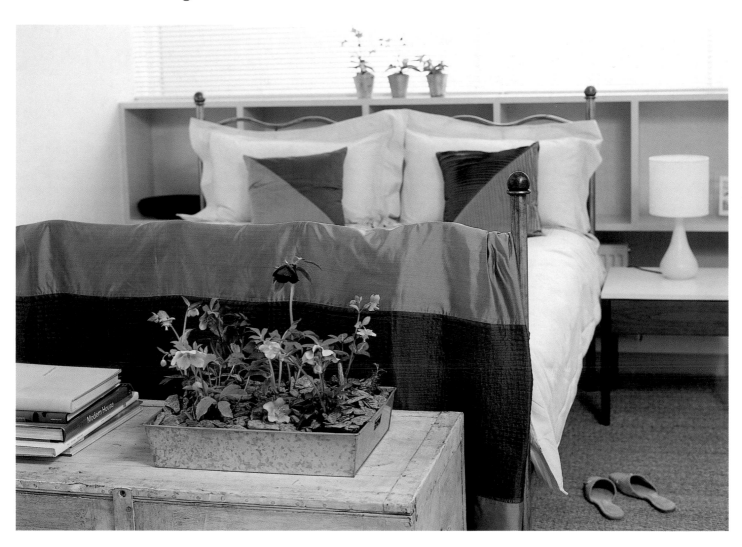

CALM SIMPLICITY

The combination of minimal furniture, clutter-free surfaces and a peaceful, deeply toned throw and cushions, adds up to a serene and peaceful bedroom. Pure white linen, almost symbolic of peaceful night's sleep down the centuries, is a good choice for the main bed linen, while colour can be introduced through accessories. These deep amethyst shades, which echo those of the charming collection of hellebores are perfect for winter, their moody tones bringing a serene warmth. The most peaceful rooms refer to nature for their colour inspiration, which is automatically in tune with what is going on outside. And this is the key to ringing the changes. As spring approaches these bedroom accessories can be changed to give softer tones of cherry blossom, lilacs and hyacinth blues.

NATURE'S TOUCH

Keeping colours muted in the bedroom makes for a serene feeling, especially if you follow a white theme. The simple lines of this white ceramic pot make a perfect contrast with the soft folds of muslin (cheesecloth), while the bold sculptural shapes of the almost black *Aeonium* 'Zwartkop' in the pot are very striking.

HARMONIOUS BALANCE

A pair of matching lamps, standing stiffly to attention either side of a willow wreath and orchids in a glass vase, makes a pleasing composition that lends this bedroom a sense of peace. With the rather formal context established by these strong elements, smaller accessories are allowed to be displayed in a less regimented way.

PAST STABILITY

Serenity relies, to a certain extent, on security, and you can create a peaceful feeling by including some accessories that have their roots in yesteryear. This little cross-stitch picture of a house might be brand new, but it has the charm of a bygone era, lending a sense of stability.

HEARTFELT MEANINGS

The heart motif is universally symbolic of love, and this picture, made from dried beans, introduces a sense of affection and security to the bedroom. Alternatively, the image of a dove, which is symbolic of peace, could be used for promoting a feeling of serenity.

candles and aromatherapy

Our love affair with candles has transcended time. Even though we live in the age of electric light and no longer have to rely on them, we appreciate their flattering light and romantic associations. This can be especially relevant in the bedroom when we want to relax away from the distractions of modern technology, and perhaps spend some quality time alone with our partners. There is a wide range of candles available to buy, including aromatherapy candles, which are delightfully scented with various essential oils. These can have various benefits, such as aiding relaxation and sleep, reducing stress or promoting a sense of well-being. The apparent mood-changing properties of various essential oils could be due to the fact that certain aromas can stimulate the brain and affect chemical balances within the body.

CANDLELIT BEDROOM
Little gold candles add sparkle to a dressing table. Positioned as these are in front of the mirror, the light is doubled by the reflection. Use just two or three for low light or more for a brighter effect.

◄ *A little tealight placed next to a bowl of water with a little essential oil added brings both light and aromatherapy benefits. The warmth of the candle encourages evaporation, so raising humidity, which benefits the skin, and releasing the aroma, benefiting your mood.*

► *A cream, ceramic double candle holder arranged with ranunculus blooms of exactly the same shades as the candles is the essence of simple purity.*

BEDTIME AROMAS

The effective ingredients in aromatherapy are the essential oils. Very costly, these are sold in tiny bottles, but you only need to use a few drops at a time. Avoid less expensive synthetic versions as these do not have the same properties as natural oils. You can use essential oils for massage, adding a few drops to a good quality but less expensive carrier, such as almond oil, or you can use them in a burner, which releases their aroma into the atmosphere. A burner consists of two parts: the lower part which accommodates a tealight, and a dish above it which is filled with water and a few drops of essential oil. The candle heats the oil and water, releasing the aroma.

◄ To unwind after a hard day, light an aromatherapy burner whilst you are still in the bathroom getting ready for bed, then take the burner with you into the bedroom to scent the air and encourage sleep. Use any of the following essential oils to reduce stress: chamomile, geranium, grapefruit, marjoram, peppermint, lemon balm or sandalwood. Cedarwood, cinnamon, geranium, jasmine, patchouli and ylang ylang are all said to be good for passion.

▲ The combination of an incense stick and aromatherapy burner fills the air with heady aromas that help to reduce stress and promote restful sleep. The smart, white frosted glass aromatherapy burner makes an elegant statement in a modern bedroom. To encourage sleep try any of the following: chamomile, frankincense, neroli or rose. Lavender is the cure-all aroma, and is useful for overcoming insomnia as well as for relaxation.

flowers in the bedroom

Vases of fresh flowers bring a little of the outside indoors, contributing a seasonal feel to the bedroom. Use them to add accent colours to your decorative scheme. If you choose seasonal flowers, their shades will always feel naturally right for the time of year and bring the room to life. Scale matters less in the bedroom than anywhere else in the house. You can use big arrangements for whole-room impact, but small posies can be just as important. A tiny vase of snowdrops or violets, for example, on a bedside or dressing table will be seen at close range. Scented flowers are always a delightful touch in the bedroom, especially near the bed.

PARADISE FOUND

If it's colour you want, there's little to beat the spectacular orange and purple bird-of-paradise plant (*Strelitzia reginae*). It won't bloom until the plant is mature (about six years old), but once it does, you can be sure of a good show. The flowers are sequential, so when one plume dies down, another pops up to replace it. It needs warmth and light, and so is perfect for a sunny bedroom.

ADD SWEET PERFUME

Bring natural perfume into the bedroom by choosing sweetly scented flowers. Paperwhite narcissus is one of the very first daffodils to come into bloom, and is certainly the most sweetly scented. Simply gather a bunch together, then place them in a plain white vase for a simple but stunning arrangement.

HEARTS AND FLOWERS

The lush abundance of ornamental cherry blossom needs little decoration or embellishment, but these pretty little raffia hearts are a very simple way to bring a romantic springtime touch to the bedroom. Tie the branches of blossom with raffia, decorate with a little raffia-bound heart, then plunge them into a pretty glass vase. Raffia is a natural material that is unaffected by water, which, happily, also magnifies the heart. The only other material you will need is garden wire.

1 Cut a length of garden wire about 30cm/12in long, and make a hook in each end to link together into a circle. Bend the circle into a heart shape.

2 Starting at the dip, bind the heart with natural raffia, tying the ends of the raffia together at the top when you get back to the starting point.

3 Tie some cherry blossom branches together with raffia, tie on the heart and plunge into the vase. Make more hearts, if you wish, to decorate the branches.

CUT FLOWERS

Fresh flowers bring instant colour. These were tied with raffia and slipped through a collar of cellophane to fill out a large vase.

LASTING COLOUR

A potted plant, such as this star-flowered *Campanula isophylla*, provides lasting colour during its flowering season.

bedroom details

Once you have finalised the general décor and large furnishings of your bedroom it is time to think about the little details and finishing touches that make the room full of your own personality. Make sure that you don't go overboard at this stage, especially if you've gone for the minimalist look – your clean, clutter-free bedroom shouldn't become a dumping ground for things that don't fit anywhere else in the house. Instead, think about pretty storage boxes, picture frames that add a splash of colour, little bags that match the colour theme of your room, as well as small tokens of special times and important people in your life.

ORGANDIE POCKETS

These simple envelopes are a very pretty way to store beautifully laundered handkerchiefs, pretty silk scarves or special gloves.

AUTUMN LEAVES

Leaves make great natural templates. Here, they have been used to decorate a stacking set of containers. The boxes were first painted in grey, then large leaves of the pin oak (*Quercus palustris*) were held in position as cream paint was stippled over using a stencil brush. The lids were further embellished with a circle of common oak leaves (*Quercus robur*).

FEATHER ARRANGEMENT

Pure white swans' feathers, displayed in a pearlized papier-mâché bowl, make a delightful memento of a special family day out. They are easy to find in the early summer near any water that is home to swans, and they make a romantic light-filtering bedroom accessory. They also look charming when tucked, like flowers, into glass vases.

BEAD WORK

Working with beads is easy, and the sparkly vibrant effect they have can brighten a room even if the item is small. These frames are a good introduction to working with beads as you simply glue the beads on to a plain bought frame. The large square frame has rocaille bead hearts and a glitter background. The round frame has bugle beads around the centre and rocaille beads round the outside, while the smallest frame has assorted beads around the sides and a glitter centre.

▶ *A bowl of sparkling baubles makes a cheery bedroom decoration. Make these for Christmas, if you like, but as they are far too good to pack away for the rest of the year, put them on display in a glass bowl. They are easy to make – just thread one or two beads on to an ordinary dressmaking pin, then push it into a ball of dry florist's foam. Repeat until the ball is completely covered, adding sequins to vary the design.*

potions and lotions

Creams, oils, tonics and potions generally come in beautiful packaging, so, rather than closet them within bedside table cupboards or drawers, let them stay out on display, bringing colour and interest to the bedroom. They look best if grouped and teamed with something larger, such as a flower arrangement, that tones with the colours of the packaging. If you prefer a rather more romantic look than that afforded by modern cosmetic packaging, collect old bottles and jars from antique stalls and fill these with the modern products. Glass always looks wonderful, but old china moisturizer jars would also add glamour to any dressing table.

COTTAGE BEDROOM

Scale is important when creating displays. This group of small bottles looks delightful on a cottage bedroom windowsill, crowned by the lace edging of a half-lowered blind. In larger rooms displays like this bring interest to niches and alcoves.

COLOUR CO-ORDINATION

If you have two or more containers of the same colour, accentuate their tones by grouping them together.

REFLECTED GLORY

Light reflecting and translucent, glass always looks glorious, whether it is old or new. It also looks great in a crowd, so group bottles against a mirror, on the bedroom mantelpiece perhaps, to double the impact of some really beautiful finds. Decant new bath and body goodies into beautiful old bottles like these, putting the purely decorative to practical use.

AROMATIC OILS

A pair of miniature glass decanters make
perfect containers for precious perfumed
oils. A scallop shell made into a candle
completes the group, making a pretty
montage for a bedroom mantel. By adding
a few drops of scented oil to the candle,
the exotic aroma is released.

COLD CREAM AND ROSES

Antique face-cream containers bring an air
of glamour to the bedroom that is perfectly
enhanced with old-fashioned roses.

MIX AND MATCH

Even disparate items can look good in a
group, as long as proportion and balance
are taken into consideration. So long as
the taller items, such as this bottle, dish
and pitcher of flowers, filter the light, they
don't dominate the smaller items.

perfumed bedrooms

A sense of well-being is about much more than the look of your surroundings. It involves all the senses, and never more so than in the bedroom. Smell is our most primitive sense and aromatherapists believe that odours can affect the chemical balances in the body, which could account for the apparent mood-changing properties of aromatic herbs such as lavender. For centuries, lavender has been prized for its calming effects, which can help to promote sleep or settle restless children, while rose oil is known to promote a feeling of well-being and to relieve nervous tension and insomnia.

FRAGRANT BEDSIDE ROSES
This summer posy includes scented garden roses, spray carnations, astrantia, great burnet and sweet cicely.

1 Sort the flowers into groups and remove thorns from the roses. Strip off any flowers or foliage that will be below the water line. Put the sweet cicely to one side.

2 Use the rest of the flowers to make the posy. Start by holding two or three of the straightest stems together, then add another stem at a 45 degree angle.

3 Turn the bouquet and add another stem at 45 degrees, laying it next to the first angled stem. Continue this way, turning the bouquet and adding subsequent stems at 45 degree angles.

4 When all the flowers are used up, use the sweet cicely to make up a collar of fronds around all the other flowers.

5 Tie the posy with raffia, then trim all the stems to the same length. Place in a vase.

▼ *Iridescent organza sachets are packed with fragrant dried rosebuds to make exotic drawer scenters.*

LOVELY LAVENDER

Keep the bedroom scented from year to year by making up a simple voile pad filled with lavender and slipping it into an elegant cover. Each summer, just replace the pad with a new one containing the latest lavender harvest.

▼ *Use royal purples and golds for an exquisite lavender cushion that is elegant enough for the most beautiful bedroom. The top layer of this cushion is made of translucent organza, which not only shows off the lavender, but allows its fragrance to be freely released into the bedroom.*

▲ *Lavender bottles make delightful scented accessories. Make them by bunching together any odd number of lavender stems. Tie the stalks tightly at the base of the flowers, then bend these over the flowers and, starting at the bent end, weave ribbon through the stems. Bind the free stems and tie the ribbons to finish.*

spicy bedroom

If sweet aromas aren't your style, try spices instead. Rich and warm, they bring an exotic ambience to the bedroom, redolent of all the mysteries of the East. Even if you do prefer sweeter scents in the summer, spices can make a refreshing change for long, dark winter nights. Cinnamon, cassia bark and cloves exude a rich, spicy, almost woody aroma; other more unusual spices, such as cardamom pods and mace, have a lighter and fresher quality. Although fresh spices can be bought in supermarkets and health food shops, the best solution is to visit the local Asian market where you will find more variety and larger quantities.

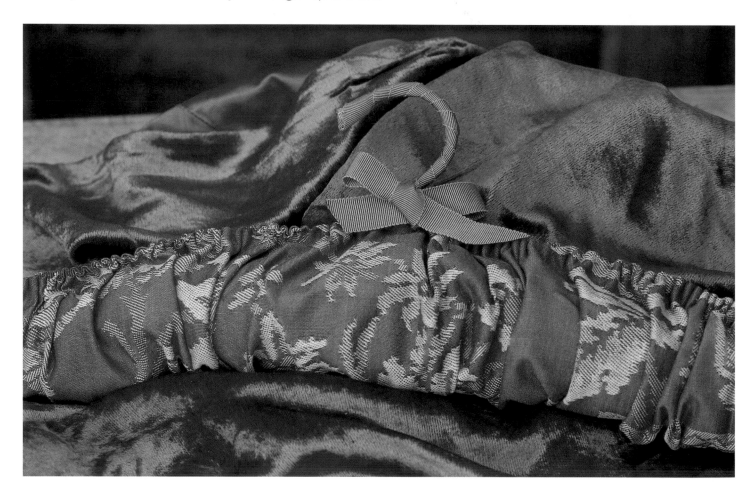

HANGING SPICES

Fill your wardrobe with the exotic scent of spices by making some padded coat hangers and filling them with cassia bark or cinnamon sticks. You won't need much fabric, so seek out luxurious remnants, such as this rich amber brocade.

◄ *Powerfully fragranced hangers can be strong enough to scent an entire room. Dressed with clothing made of beautiful fabric, they can become a feature.*

▶ *Heart-shaped hanging sachets filled with cinnamon make spicy, aromatic alternatives to lavender bags.*

SPICED SACHETS

The traditional way to bring spicy scents into the bedroom is with sachets and bags. These lace-edged handkerchiefs are given a new lease of life tied into sachets with silk ribbon and filled with spices.

▼ *This gloriously sensuous taffeta cushion, adorned with generous golden tassels, is filled with cardamom and fennel. The spices show through the transparent mesh top layer of the cushion, and just need a quick shake to release the fragrances.*

▲ *A much smaller cardamom-filled sachet, made from a rich combination of shot organza, velvet and chenille, makes a spicy alternative to the traditional lavender bag, and can be tucked into drawers to delicately scent lingerie.*

bathrooms

Your bathroom might be a tiny corner space in which there is barely any room, or it might be one of the largest rooms in the house, but whatever its size the function is the same. This is the home spa; the pleasure zone where we can luxuriate and pamper away the stresses of life. Take care when choosing the fittings, as you could be living with them for a while. Once the essentials are in place you can start to include the finishing touches, by adding colour with paint, towels and accessories, and stocking it with exquisite bath oils, and luxurious soaps

start with **white**

Bathrooms can be large and luxurious, or small and minimalist, but whatever shape or size it is, you will have to fit basically the same amount of bathroom furniture inside. This can be quite an achievement so you will need to make sure the bathroom suite you choose is one you can live with for some time. It is wise to choose bathroom suites in white or cream, which won't date and can be adapted and personalized through the use of coloured accessories.

COLOUR UPDATE

Splashes of bright colour revive a traditional bathroom. Cherry-red towels and architectural potted plants add a quick-fix fashion element to a pure white background.

PALE TONES

Beautiful stone in sleek lines is the ultimate material for a modern bathroom. Here, it has been teamed with clear glass shelves to bring a light airy feel to a minute bathroom. The wall-mounted hand basin has made clever use of what would have been dead space at the end of the bath.

SEA TONES

A classic white basin with traditional chrome taps takes on a contemporary look with the addition of diagonally laid wall tiles, which have been stamped with a smart sea-green marine theme. Towels with a starfish motif complement the décor.

STAMPING ON COLOUR

Little beats traditional stamping for bringing an instant decorative touch to any room. In this example a row of diamonds is being applied above a tiled section of wall. Once you have found the right design of stamp, the procedure is very straightforward. All that is needed is masking tape, a brush, a plate, emulsion (latex) paint and a small foam roller.

1 Stick a length of masking tape along the top edge of the moulding or the top of the tiles. This will give you a straight line to stamp along.

2 Mark the position of the stamp in pencil on the back of the block, so you can see where to place it.

3 Spread some emulsion (latex) paint on to a plate, run a small foam roller through it until it is evenly coated.

4 Roll paint on to the stamp and press it on the wall, making sure all the stamp has even pressure.

5 Line up the pencil mark on the block with the edge of the previous print for each print, so that your stamps meet but don't overprint.

▶ *Use a colour link to give continuity of style. Here, silver-grey coronets stencilled on to the tiles are echoed by simple motifs applied in the same colour on the lace-edged hand towels. Silver-grey is an excellent colour choice for motifs in a bathroom that is equipped with shiny chrome bath and basin taps.*

CLASSIC COLOUR

This original Victorian claw-foot bath, painted in nineteenth-century racing green, provides the focus in this large traditional bathroom. The challenge was to find a paint colour for the walls that was both sympathetic to the beautiful old stripped wooden floors and window frames, while bringing a lighter, more modern feel to the room. Exquisite celadon green does the trick, while setting off the reproduction brass taps and the original brass towel rail. A tall papyrus in the corner adds a striking finishing touch to the room.

natural tones

Neutral colours look wonderful in a bathroom. They retain a fresh feel while softening sharp shiny white, which is virtually compulsory in smart modern bathrooms. Neutral colours also provide plenty of scope for using natural materials, such as limed wood, bentwood, cane and basketry, all of which offer a suitably beach-like feel that is so compatible with the watery environment of the bathroom. For accessories, add piles of pebbles, carefully positioned shells and corals as well as the more practical sponges and loofahs. If you want to add a little extra colour, one of the best choices is blue, reminiscent of sea and sky.

NEUTRAL TILES

This tiny bathroom takes on a smart look with the help of neutral mosaics, which have been used on the walls, floor and to box in the bath. The neutral shade gives the room an exclusive look, while ensuring it will not date. Natural wood accessories add the perfect finishing touch. Neutral colours transcend time, blending, as they do, with nature, very often becoming even more beautiful as they age. The ashy tones of driftwood, weathered by sun and salt, also look wonderful in a bathroom.

WOODEN BATHMAT

Duckboard painted with yacht varnish will stay smart for years and can easily be made into an ideal self-draining bathmat. Simply cut slats and two end pieces to length. Sand all the ends and varnish all round before screwing together from the underside; countersink the screws so they don't protrude.

MODERN PLUS NEUTRALS

Clear or translucent shower curtains and screens teamed with neutral colours and natural materials add a contemporary touch to a bathroom. In small bathrooms and shower rooms, clear plastic also creates a sense of space. This transparent PVC (vinyl) curtain efficiently protects the rest of the room against splashes, without visually dividing what is already a small space. It is also an attractive item that suits a more modern bathroom.

RECYCLED WOOD

Old orange boxes can be turned into useful bathroom shelving, even if they're more than a little damaged. Small scale shelves like these above a basin are the perfect proportion for small bathroom paraphernalia, such as toothbrushes, toothpaste and spare soaps. Break the boxes up and cut the pieces down to balance the width of the basin, then nail them back together.

BENTWOOD AND WHITE

A blue and white seat brings colour to a beautiful old cane and bentwood chair that with age has taken on the look of bleached driftwood. Fresh white shower robes and blue-striped towels help to make the most of the neutral tones of the wood and cane. Blue and white is a traditional combination that works well with neutral colours and natural materials, and its classic appeal is equally timeless.

bathroom **drapes**

Wherever drapes are used, they lend softness and colour to a room, and for this reason, they offer plenty of decorating scope. However, they also have more practical uses: at windows, curtains and blinds protect privacy, block out the light and in the case of sheers, disguise an outlook that is less than beautiful. Many bathrooms have shower curtains whose primary purpose is to keep shower water in its proper place, but which can also be used to protect privacy. They also divide the space. An opaque shower curtain visually reduces the bathroom's size; the more translucent or transparent it is, the more open the room will look, which can be important in a small bathroom.

RIBBON-TIED BLIND

This simple blind is perfect for a tall window where it is left tied up all the time. It looks sophisticated, but is very easy to make. Choose any lightweight fabric to suit your colour scheme and some 5cm/2in wide ribbon in a complementary shade. Self-adhesive fabric tape makes the job really easy. The only fixing required is to screw a wooden batten (furring strip) to the top of the window frame, for which you will need a drill.

1 Cut two pieces of fabric the size of the finished blind plus a 3cm/1¼in seam allowance all round. With right sides together, stitch the two pieces along three sides, leaving the top open. Trim the corners, turn through, then ease them out. Press the edges.

2 Turn in and baste the top edge. Cut a piece of self-adhesive fabric tape to fit the width of the blind, then stitch the sewing side to the back of the blind.

3 Cut two pieces of ribbon, each twice the length of the blind plus 20cm/8in. Stitch one piece one-quarter in from one edge of the blind, so that half the ribbon falls down the back and half down the front. Repeat with the other ribbon on the other side.

4 Screw the batten to the top of the window frame and fix the sticking side of the fabric tape to this. Stick the blind into position. Gather up the blind to the desired height and use the ribbons to tie it.

NEOCLASSICAL URN

For a stylish, classical look paint a design on to a plain white or cream roller blind. This neoclassical urn was traced off the drapes that surround the window, then enlarged on a photocopier so it could be traced on to the blind. Finally, it was painted using fabric paints. A roller blind is perfect for a functional bathroom, but can be a bit stark; drapes soften the effect without being over-fussy.

VICTORIAN WINDOW

For a tiny bathroom window it is better to forget about curtains or even blinds, and use some other method of adding privacy without excluding any light. This idea comes from the etched glass windows of the Victorian era, and is easily achieved using car enamel paint. It gives a lovely frosty look to a window and suits a bathroom very well. You will need a stencil card with your chosen design, masking tape, brown paper, and matt white car enamel spray.

1 Tape the stencil card in position. Protect the surrounding area using brown paper and masking tape. Make sure you cover a large area around the stencil as the spray might go further than you think.

2 Shake the paint can thoroughly, then spray from a distance of at least 30cm/12in in short puffs. Allow to dry before removing the stencil and paper.

A ROW OF MERMAIDS

There is an enormous range of shower curtains available, and it is easy to find a style or design to suit any bathroom décor, but consider making your own. This happy mermaid design on a length of muslin (cheesecloth), which has been dyed a soft green and lined with PVC (vinyl), makes a softly sumptuous drape.

CURTAIN POCKETS

Adding pockets to a PVC (vinyl) shower curtain provides space either for practical paraphernalia such as shower gels, or for decorative ideas, as here. Translucent PVC doesn't affect the light airy feel of the room, yet by changing the contents of the pockets, you can transform the whole colour scheme and ambience.

bathroom blues

The combination of china blue and white is a perennial favourite in the bathroom. It is a fresh clean look that can always be added to with both antique and modern towels and accessories. Whether you use mainly blue or mainly white is a matter of personal choice, though clever scheming can enhance the proportions of the bathroom. Small bathrooms can be opened up by being painted mainly in white and given touches of blue, while larger spaces can look cosier when given more generous splashes of blue. If in doubt, err on the mainly white side with the sanitaryware for a streamlined look and add blue with accessories.

STRIPES OF BLUE

White and blue stripes give a fresh colour scheme. Even if your bathroom is painted white throughout, you can bring in some blue stripes with towels and flannels.

▼ *When teaming several blues, use a minimum of three different shades. If you put two together that don't quite go, it can look like a mistake. Three or more always fit happily together.*

▲ *Use a combination of paint effects to add a new look to your bathroom. This wall has been very subtly sponged on the lower half to make the most of the direct light it receives. The top half of the wall reverses the colours so that the pale colour is the most dominant. A row of pretty stencilled stars holds the contrasting tones and creates some decorative detail. The bathroom accessories have been carefully chosen to complement the décor and not detract from it.*

BLUE-STAINED FLOORS

If your budget doesn't run to real wooden boards, you can use strips of hardwood painted to look like real wood instead. Buy sufficient 6mm/¼in hardboard sheets to cover your bathroom floor and cut them into 15cm/6in wide boards. The painted-wood effect is achieved by working a tool called a wood-graining comb through wet paint. Here the boards are painted china blue, but obviously other colours could work well depending on your overall scheme. Gaps between the boards need to be sealed with flexible acrylic sealant and the whole floor is finished with quick-drying satin varnish.

1 Paint a board with a thick coat of off-white emulsion (latex) paint, and, while the paint is still wet, run the wood-graining comb down the length. Repeat with the other boards and leave to dry.

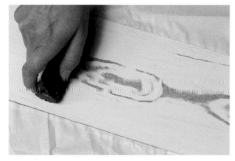

2 In a paint kettle, mix china blue matt emulsion (latex) paint with water to the consistency of cream, then paint a thin coat on to the 'grained' boards. Allow the paint to dry.

3 Rub over the boards with fine-grade sandpaper to remove the wash from the 'grain' underneath. Wipe the boards with a damp cloth then seal each one with a coat of quick-drying satin varnish. Allow the varnish to dry.

4 Cut the boards to size and lay them out on the floor, leaving a small gap between the boards. Lay the floor using 2cm/¾in oblong nails. Use a nail punch to sink each nail head below the surface. Seal the gaps between boards with flexible acrylic sealant. Use a damp sponge to smooth the sealant and wipe away any excess.

5 Finally, paint the floor with two coats of quick-drying satin varnish, allowing it to dry completely between coats.

marine themes

Fishy themes suit the watery environment of bathrooms, and, thankfully, they include endless simple motifs that are easy to do. Fish, shells, starfish and seahorses are all beautiful, and can be used as single bold motifs or repeated for an all-over design. Simple outlines can be painted directly on to walls and fabrics, or stamped or stencilled. If you are adept with a paintbrush, you could try more painterly designs, reminiscent of illustrations found in Victorian natural science books, or look for out-of-copyright designs in art shops, which you can cut out and stick on to pieces of furniture that have been previously painted and aged.

FISHY DECORATION

Use watery motifs and clearest mint green to decorate a pretty bathroom cabinet.

1 Rub down the surface of the cupboard with sandpaper and wipe off any dust. Paint with light cream paint, allow to dry thoroughly, then rub down again to reveal some of the grain. Paint the moulding and door frame in light green. Allow to dry and sand as before.

2 Cut out fish motifs and fix in place using watered-down PVA (white) glue. Press in place, ensuring the edges are firmly fixed and the surface is smooth. Wipe away excess glue from around the motif and allow to dry.

3 When the glue is completely dry, varnish the whole cupboard with a coat of non-yellowing artist's dead flat varnish. Allow it to dry completely before applying further coats of varnish, until the surface feels totally smooth.

◀ *This pair of freshwater fish was cut from a sheet of wrapping paper and glued into position. The weed was hand-painted.*

NAUTILUS MOTIFS

Large shells make beautiful subjects for bathroom decoration. Their strong shapes have been popular motifs for centuries, so there are plenty out-of-copyright images available for use as decoupage.

SEA-STAMPED BATHROOM

These clean, clear stamp designs keep the freshness of a white bathroom, but prevent it looking stark by adding a controlled amount of colour. Choose stamps that are large enough to create a bold design. Here, blue shells rotate on the curtain to give a pleasingly random pattern. Delicate golden seahorses, starfish and shells add a touch of sunshine to the walls. For a sun-bleached look, give walls a light wash with watered-down white emulsion (latex) paint which makes all the sharp contrasts disappear and gives a calming finish.

STARFISH MIRROR

Starfish and shells are such simple motifs they are easy to draw freehand on to frames, furniture and even walls. This simple distressed white frame has been given golden motifs to bring sparkle to the bathroom. It works especially well if you have chosen brass taps, tying in the colour without becoming too garish. If you have chrome taps, paint the motifs in silver.

beachcomber's paradise

Beaches are an irresistible treasure trove. Once down on the beach, you won't be able to stop picking up all those perfect little shells, pebbles, gorgeous pieces of driftwood, bits of seaweed, and even the odd fossil. It is compulsive hunting, and pockets and bags are soon filled with wonderful finds. Beaches are most productive in winter, when stormy seas throw up generous amounts of bounty – and there are fewer hunters to bag them. When you get home, turn them into wonderful accessories for the bathroom, where they will look at home with all the water.

WINDOW SCREEN

This is an ideal screen for any window that isn't overlooked, as its main purpose is to act as a decorative foil, and an individual way of displaying seashore finds. Everything – worn glass, shells, stones, fishing floats, weights and lures – are fixed on near-invisible fishing line, so the screen appears to float in mid-air within the window space. The more you gaze at it the more the image of the sea is bought to mind. Fix the items on to the line by making holes in them, tying them or using a glue gun. Once you have several lines of objects, fix them to a length of dowel cut the same width as the window. The best way to fix the lines is to tie them to rings, which are then hung from hooks screwed into the dowel. This gives the lines more flexibility so that the objects dance and swing in the slightest breeze.

DRIFTWOOD SHELVES

This set of hanging shelves is perfect for a beach-style bathroom, and you couldn't wish for a better display unit for your beachcombing finds. The shelves are made from bits of planking found on a beach after a storm, but cut-down floorboards would do just as well. String the boards together with window sash cord, or some old rope for an even more authentic beachcombing look. Before they were assembled, these boards were given a weathered look with a coat of dilute white emulsion (latex) paint. Make sure the shelves are hanging in a place where they won't be bumped into or disturbed, as they are quite finely balanced. Once you have fixed the shelves in position, arrange your most exquisite finds or other natural objects on them. Choose items that have interesting and delicate shapes. Don't overfill the shelves, keep it simple.

DECORATIVE FINDS

The items that you find when beach-combing can be dual-purpose in the bathroom, large shells can act as a soap dish or can hold bath crystals. They can also be purely decorative. Here an old enamel bowl filled with shells has a lovely seaside holiday look.

▶ *If you have an extensive collection of shells make the most of them with a shell-decorated basket, set amongst a display of larger shells. The basket can also make a pretty but practical container for soaps, shampoos or bottles of bath oil.*

PRACTICAL FINDS

The thin planks used to make orange boxes are often found singly on the beach, but if you need more ask your greengrocer for a discarded box. These blinds work best on small windows.

▲ *Driftwood can be used to make delightful bathroom fittings and accessories. Here, the wood has been made into a wonderful organic mirror frame with a co-ordinating bathroom cabinet. The big scallop shells with their distinctive colour and shape are used judiciously as a restrained decoration.*

▲ *Thin mirror with a seaside theme makes an ideal bathroom fixture. Simply collect some shells on the seashore or from local fishmongers and attach them to a plain wooden frame using a glue gun. Make up striking designs by choosing contrasting shells in almost white and charcoal grey, then fixing them in alternate rows.*

celestial themes

If your favourite time to luxuriate in the bath is just before going to bed, a magical starry theme makes ideal inspiration for the décor. Star motifs are easy to find and easy to make up in template form, giving you endless scope for decoration. They can be stencilled, stamped or used as decoupage, either in all-over fashion, or as a focal point in the bathroom. If your style is more minimal than decorative, keep the motifs to smaller fixtures, such as shelves or a cabinet.

▲ A HEAVENLY BOUDOIR

If you love to spend time in the bath turn your bathing into an art form and your bathroom into a boudoir. This heavenly bath would tempt you to spend hours in it and the muslin drape gives a light and pretty effect that is pure fantasy. Mouldings picked out in white against the cream walls give the impression of panelling, and white-painted floors carry through the light-reflecting colour scheme. The stars on the drapes, which create the ultimate celestial effect, are repeated on the bath and chair cushion. The bath has gold taps and feet to match.

▶ *Choose your accessories with care for this kind of bathroom. The impact of the theme will work much better if it is restricted to a few items.*

HEAVENLY WALLS

Plaster has a powdery quality and a pure white colour, which make it an especially interesting wall embellishment. When it is teamed with the palest background colour and white furniture, the bathroom takes on an almost ethereal, cloudy quality. The mouled plaster motifs can be bought in various shapes and sizes.

1 To help you decide where to place the plaster motifs, make full-size photocopies of them first and experiment with them, using small pieces of masking tape to attach them to the wall.

2 Seal the plaster stars with clear varnish or PVA (white) glue mixed with water.

3 When the stars are dry, use wall adhesive to attach them to the walls. Use a wood offcut as a spacer for positioning them at regular intervals.

▼ *Another heavenly theme is provided by these little classical cherubs, which add a fanciful note to a simple bathroom cabinet. The cupboard was coloured with a soft grey woodstain before the cherub motifs were stamped on in gold paint.*

STAR-STUDDED CUPBOARD

Finish a wooden cabinet with metal door panels that have been decorated with punched star shapes.

space-sensitive bathrooms

It is quite likely that your bathroom is severely limited by space. This doesn't mean, however, that you can't tailor it to suit your decorative desires, you just have to be bit cleverer about planning the space. The same colour principles apply to large and small bathrooms – white sanitaryware is currently almost mandatory for any self-respecting bathroom, and fresh clean hues such as aqua or blue always work, as do natural colours such as white, cream and neutrals.

OPENING UP DOORS

In a small bathroom in a family home you will increase the sense of space if you exchange a single door for louvred ones, which take less space on opening and add a feeling of lightness. This is an especially effective idea if your toilet is an annexe of the bathroom, rather than directly off a landing. Painting the doors and picking out the porthole window in blue gives this bathroom a Mediterranean tone.

KEEP THINGS SIMPLE

Simplicity is the best way to make the most of a small bathroom. Paint the walls white and consider a door that opens outwards on to the landing rather than inwards. A traditional blue and white striped towel hanging on a towel roller on the back of the door suits the retro look of this bathroom, and also saves space.

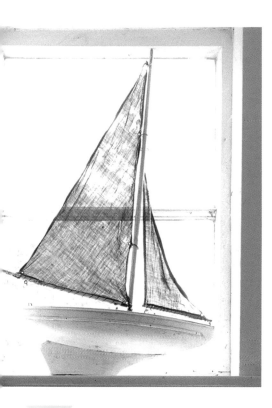

A TINY WINDOW

Small windows might not let in huge amounts of light, but, if they are high up like this one, you can make the maximum use of the light that passes through them. Way out of range of prying eyes, you can use clear glass instead of the more usual light-restricting textured bathroom glass. You can also dispense with light-blocking curtains and use a decorative item instead, such as this model yacht, to add a personal touch to the window.

NIFTY NICHES

If you have any little alcoves or niches, fit some shelves into them and use them for beachcombing finds or other natural-look ornaments. If storage space is limited you can forget the decorative items and use them to store your hand or guest towels, jars of soaps or other bathtime luxuries. But even this can be made into a pretty feature if you keep the towels white and weigh them down with some lovely big smooth sea stones.

SIMPLE DETAILS

You need to keep clutter to a minimum in a small bathroom. Turn every nook and cranny into a cupboard or enclosure so you have plenty of storage space. Fortunately, the majority of bathroom paraphernalia is made up of small bottles, packets and tubes, which can be stored in the smallest of spaces. Even if space is tight, you will need a few pretty things to stop the bathroom looking too stark. Just one or two, such as these home-made flower waters, is all you need. Anything translucent works well because it gives a feeling of light and space in a small room while adding a decorative touch.

storage ideas

There's always a certain amount of clutter in a bathroom. Some of it is gorgeous, like soaps and bottles of bath oil, and even sponges, brushes and loofahs can look wonderful displayed on shelves. Other things, such as toothbrushes, half-squeezed tubes of toothpaste, medicines, sticking plasters and shavers, aren't quite so lovely, so are best hidden behind cupboard doors. Aim for as much storage space as you can, though think carefully how you want to arrange it. If your bathroom cupboards happen to be large, you could stack them with boxes or baskets filled with things-of-a-kind to make finding them easy.

PRETTY USEFUL

As well as providing valuable storage space, open shelves are a wonderful opportunity for displaying practical bathroom accessories as visually attractive objects. Stacked towels bring colour to the bathroom, either emphasizing the current scheme, or, like fashion accessories, giving you the option of quick changes with the seasons. Choose wonderful spring greens with soft lilac-hyacinth shades for spring; seaside blues and whites for summer; soft mossy greens with russet for autumn; and berry reds in winter. Quite apart from their content, shelves themselves can be a decorative feature in the bathroom. Making excellent use of a narrow alcove, these examples have attractively scalloped fronts, which give an added decorative touch. Painted white, they make a perfect framework for the folded towels and other accessories they hold.

WIRE BATH TIDY

This wire tidy is ideal for storing sponges and loofahs that should dry out between use. You need small-gauge chickenwire, natural raffia and protective gloves.

1 Using wire cutters, cut a 50cm/20in length of chickenwire. Fold the wire in half so that the smooth ends meet Turn in the cut ends and press flat.

2 To define the sides of the tidy, fold in 7.5cm/3in all around and press flat. Open out the folds so that they stand at 90°. To form the corners, pinch the exces wire into a point, then fold flat into the sides.

3 With raffia, work running stitches around the edge of the tidy. Tie a reef knot at each corner, where the lengths of raffia meet.

DECORATING WITH DECOUPAGE

This is an easy way to give junk shop furniture and accessories new life. Literally meaning 'the process of cutting', the technique involves cutting out beautiful printed images or shapes from paper and sticking them decoratively on to an object – anything from a flat board or a box to a piece of furniture. The finished item is finally varnished. Several coats of matt acrylic non-yellowing artist's varnish are applied until the motifs look as if they have been hand-painted. Images can be taken from any illustrated source, such as old magazines, wallpaper, wrapping paper, or specially produced books.

1 First prepare the item to be decorated. If the paint is in good condition, sand it to key the surface, then wipe it down with warm soapy water and leave to dry. Paintwork that is in poor condition has to be completely stripped off, and then the piece will have to be repainted.

HANG IT UP

Use hooks and rails on the walls to hang towels, soaps on ropes and drawstring bags of bathroom clutter. You will get things out of the way and create a decorative element. This charming set of boat hooks works particularly well.

STORAGE BUCKET

Give a galvanized bucket a decoupage decoration of scallop shells to transform it from the mundane to the stylish, and then use it for storage. The design needs to be sealed with varnish, applied to the whole bucket exterior.

2 Using a pair of small sharp scissors, cut out your chosen images, then plan how they will be arranged.

3 Glue each image into position, using watered-down PVA (white) glue. Press down in the centre and work outwards to spread the glue. Leave for a few minutes, then wipe away any excess glue with a sponge. Allow to dry.

TUCK IT ALL AWAY

Hide unsightly bathroom items such as tubes of ointment and cleaning products in attractive small cabinets rather than have them in public view. Here the top is used to display a gorgeous drawstring bag, filled with fragrant lavender.

4 Stir the varnish well and apply a thin coat. Allow to dry, then gently sand using fine sandpaper. Apply further coats until the piece is smooth.

plants in the bathroom

Bring life to the bathroom with vibrant green potted plants and flowers. Choose those that enjoy a damp, misty environment, such as ferns or jungle plants. Ferns are an excellent choice as they can survive in fairly low light levels and there are plenty of varieties to choose from. Marginal aquatic plants also make a good choice for the bathroom, though many need to have wet roots at all times, so keep a few inches of water in the planter that holds their container. Plants with form and shape are ideal as they bring an element of organic sculpture. In small bathrooms, a stunning plant or group of plants is all you need in terms of decorative interest.

SPIKY POTS

The wonderful spiky look of grasses makes a smart display, especially if you plant up several pots and place them in serried ranks on the bathroom windowsill. Potted in brightly coloured bowls and mulched with white pebbles, they make a fun, organic bathroom feature. Choose varieties that stand up straight. This club rush (*Isolepsis cernua*) is perfect.

BATHROOM LILIES

Arum lilies (*Zantedeschia*) are marginal plants, so love water and dampness. With exquisite tubular flowers, they are extremely elegant, and their sheer size makes a dramatic, almost theatrical statement. Here they have been planted in large galvanized containers for a smart modern look.

DRAPING IVY

Trailing ivies grow happily in moist atmospheres with low light levels, and therefore are good bathroom plants. Their foliage colours make particularly striking contrasts against white. Look for the more attractive varieties with tiny, finely cut leaves and pretty silver-green colour.

FLOWER POSIES

Vases of cut flowers offer a good solution for anyone who is diffident about their indoor plant-care skills. Here, posies of delicate silkweed (*Asclepias*) have been tucked into five silver pots to make a striking bathroom arrangement. These are quick to do, yet very effective, and the idea can be reproduced with any small flowers to bring a seasonal touch to the bathroom at any time of the year.

bathroom accessories

Decorative details can transform the plainest bathroom into one that is undeniably yours. The joy of bathroom decoration is that many practical accessories – soap dishes or toothbrush mugs – are lovely in themselves, so you can use these functional items to make your bathroom beautiful. Decorative additions don't have to be useful, however, embellish your bathroom with items that are there purely for their beauty or colour, or simply because you enjoy looking at them.

USE NATURE'S ARTWORK

Make your own bathroom montage. Sea beauties – shells, sand dollars and sea anemones – look stunning simply tipped into clear glass tanks.

SPARKLING SILVER

These old-fashioned silver accessories look stunning set against the clean simplicity of fresh white towels. The black decorative detail on one of the towels lends strong definition to the whole colour scheme. When you have a lot of small accessories, it is possible to retain a cohesive look by limiting them to the same colour group. Black and white is monotone, but the addition of silver injects welcome sparkle and lends a sense of luxury to the whole bathroom.

LINEN LAUNDRY BAGS

Baskets have replaced old-fashioned laundry bags, but these beautiful traditional linen bags take up much less space and are far nicer to look at. Hung from an antique towel rail they are a delightful storage solution. Use natural fibres, such as cotton or linen or, alternatively, old thick-weave cotton towels, which can still be bought from antique shops that specialize in fabrics. For a really classy flourish, decorate each one with an embroidered initial.

OLD CHINA BLUES

Blue and white china works wonderfully well in the watery ambience of the bathroom and evokes feelings of a bygone age. Individual items don't even have to match, for no matter how different the patterns may be, the pieces always look good together. Vary the scale of the patterns, mixing, for example, pieces decorated with large motifs with those incorporating small all-over designs. This type of china has been popular since it first began to be imported from China centuries ago. It was produced by the wagonload in the past, so is not difficult to find on antique stalls and in junk shops, and is a fun style to collect. Look out for soap dishes, large bowls and jars, which can be framed to provide a coherent scheme for the whole bathroom.

CREAMY HUES

Stay true to one colour only and keep even your accessories strictly toning with pure whites or creams. This will give you a bathroom of stylish calm.

SHINY REFLECTIONS

Mirrors and plenty of silver accessories bring reflections to bathrooms, which increase the light levels and create a greater feeling of space. Add sheeny fabrics like silk, satin and ribbons for extra reflections. This toilet bag in shiny silk, satin and ribbon, incorporates organza ribbon panels filled with whole cardamom pods, which exude an exotic perfume that pervades the entire bathroom.

pampering products

Luscious scented oils and unguents have always been associated with the pleasures of bathing. Nowadays, we are offered an ever-widening choice of bath and body products. Many come in beautiful packaging, though if you have your own favourite bottles or containers, decanting toiletries into them can give your bathroom an individual look. As well as perfumes, oils, soaps and bath crystals, you can bring gloriously perfumed flowers in from the garden to introduce fresh seasonal scent into the bathroom.

BATHSIDE DISPLAY

Evoke the glamour of yesteryear by decanting bath crystals into beautiful old cut-glass bottles, then group them for impact. This will make a beautiful array for special pampering sessions for yourself, or for a guest bathroom. Enhance the display further by decorating it with dramatic flower stems or bunches of dried herbs on your visitors' arrival.

▶ *If you want to keep true to your chosen colour theme, buy your own pots and bottles and transfer your favourite creams and lotions into them.*

▲ *Display rose bath crystals in bowls enjoy their exquisite perfume even be you get into the bath. The pretty colo sparkle also makes an attractive sho*

SCENTED OILS

A bouquet of huge old-fashioned roses forms a backdrop to a pleasing group of exquisite crystal bottles. The heady scent of the flowers is a perfect accompaniment for a self-pampering session.

ELEGANT BOTTLES

If you would rather have a clean uncluttered look in your bathroom use fewer items and give a simple and appealing look by displaying just a few antique cork-stoppered bottles.

LAVENDER WREATH

A wreath of sweet fresh lavender will retain its shape as it gradually dries out. Hang one up in the bathroom and enjoy its distinctive fragrance until next year's lavender harvest.

the outside room

Transform the garden into an outdoor room; make it into a green idyll where you can find peace amongst plants and flowers, well away from household chores and the pressures of modern living. This is your closest contact with nature, where you can be in touch with the seasons as the garden bursts into activity in spring, blooms in summer, brings golden harvest in autumn, and peacefully sleeps in winter. Cleverly planned, even the smallest patio or yard can offer a surprising amount of space for relaxing on your own, or with friends and family.

paths and floors

Make pathways a priority when planning the layout of your outdoor space. Once these and related hard features, such as decking and patios, are in place, the foundation of your garden will be established. Whereas indoors a seamless wall-to-wall floor finish maximizes the sense of space in a room, outside you need to plan for variety. Create interesting vistas by combining different elements such as brick or pebble paths with a paved patio or wooden decking plus an interesting ground detail or two. A well-thought-out garden floor always appears elegant and interesting, even before the addition of a single plant, so your garden will look good even while you are waiting for shrubs and perennials to grow and mature.

PLAN BRICK PATHS

Use paths to define planting areas in a lawn-free, potager-style garden that encompasses distinct areas for growing herbs, flowers, fruits and vegetables. Although the planting in this lush garden is informal and exuberant, the pathways provide a regular structure and give the whole design an architectural quality. The main path leads the eye naturally down through the vegetation to an inviting, brightly painted focal point seat.

COOL CRAZY PAVING

Crazy paving might be a 1960s cliché, but done well, it can make a very effective and original pathway that becomes a feature in itself. Here, roughly hewn slates have been laid flat and embedded in concrete. For the edging, the same slates have been stacked horizontally and vertically, giving the impression of dry-stone walls. The result is an interesting textural combination that retains a continuity because the same material has been used throughout.

AN ALPINE FLOOR FEATURE

Even in a tiny garden, a pathway sometimes need a hub – a point at which paths meet or change direction. This is a good place to plan a feature – a circle of pebbles set in concrete, perhaps, or even something more elaborate and plant related. This wheel structure, made of bricks and an old drain cover, provides a form for a miniature garden of spreading alpines or rock garden plants. You wouldn't want people to walk over this, but you could use it as a focal point to run the paths around – like a decorative roundabout. Rock garden plants are not difficult to look after, although true alpines are damp-sensitive and need plenty of gravel to assure good drainage. Gravel, slate and large pebbles were used here to create an interesting surface, over which the plants will eventually spread to create a rich tapestry, to gradually colonize.

This wheel is about 250cm/8ft in diameter and required 62 bricks, but you can make yours as small or as large as you like, depending on the space you want to fill. You can calculate the number of plants you need by checking their spread on the plant label; allow about three alpines with a 30cm/12in spread per section. In this wheel, each section has been planted with a different variety, so that as they grow, they will help to define the design.

1 Dig over the approximate area of the wheel and prepare the earth by adding compost and fertilizer.

2 Make a simple pair of compasses from a piece of string the length of the wheel's radius, with a short stake tied to each end. Push one stake into the ground, and use the other to mark the circle. Place a drain cover in the centre.

3 Place bricks around the edge of the circle and along the 'spokes'.

4 Position the plants as desired. Sprinkle gravel between and around the plants to cover the earth and finish the design with decorative pebbles and slates.

▼ *Don't worry if a mini alpine garden looks a little thin on the ground when you first plant it; alpines spread remarkably quickly in the summer, so it will very soon fill out.*

adding ground **interest**

Detail on the ground pays huge dividends in the garden, because whatever the season it is always on view. In winter, when herbaceous borders die down, it becomes the dominant element, so by adding decorative touches to patios and special corners, or near pathways and ponds, you will introduce all-year interest. Even something as simple as a few boulders can make a difference, becoming more overgrown in summer, but providing simple sculpture in winter. Alternatively, you could make mini gardens, or even an elaborate floor feature.

▲ COLOURFUL MOSAIC

Incorporated into a patio, this colourful outdoor 'rug' brings year-round interest to a paved area near the house, where it can be admired through a window even in the depths of winter. It makes use of small pebbles collected from around the garden and various recycled materials, such as pieces of old slate, broken garden terracotta pots and discarded china pot lids. The design needs to be laid on to a prepared concrete base, so if you are having your patio paved, get the contractors to provide a concrete and aggregate flatbed about 10cm/4in deep, allowing a 5cm/2in clearance below the level of the rest of the paving.

The whole design needs to be completed in a single dry day, before the mortar begins to set. Before you start, make sure you have assembled all the necessary materials and tools: cement and sand for bedding the materials, a straightedge, a small hammer, a soft brush and a watering can. Mortar colour mixed into the final dressing will ensure that the mosaic materials are shown off to best effect.

1 Prepare the mortar bedding by mixing equal quantities of sharp sand and cement. Pour this dry mix over the flatbed, using a straightedge to smooth it flat. Scrape away a little from the centre so the mix doesn't overflow as you work.

2 Start laying the design from the outside and work towards the centre, using a small hammer to tap the pebbles and other materials into position.

3 When the design is finished, brush dry mortar, mixed with mortar colour if you are using it, evenly around the stones. Dampen the entire surface to set the mortar, using a watering can fitted with a fine sprinkler.

4 Protect the mosaic for three days by covering it with a board raised on four bricks and overlaid with a waterproof sheet. Don't walk on the mosaic for one month to allow the mortar to set fully.

BOULDER INTEREST

Huge smooth boulders make a focal point
by the side of a large wildlife pond, lending
importance to the gravel pathway. Their
smooth rock surfaces provide visual relief
against these busy and rather untidy
grass-like marginal plants. These particular
boulders have the added interest of
contrast stripes and patterns.

A SCENTED CARPET

A miniature potted thyme garden brings
ground level interest to a corner of the
garden. The pots themselves, arranged in
a circular form, provide structure that is
retained even through the winter. Stacked
spare pots lend extra height, sculptural
interest and terracotta tone to the whole
ensemble. As well as being a visual
delight, this garden within a garden has a
practical element, too. Thyme spreads
enthusiastically, and can soon take up
huge tracts of space. By growing it in pots,
you can keep it under control.

MAKE A SHELL EDGING

Scallop shells in soft coral shades make a
delightful soft edging for terracotta-
coloured paving. Resilient enough to
withstand winter weather, they will look
good even when the summer greenery has
died down. Fishmongers sell scallops in
their complete shells, so if you like shellfish
you can eat and collect.

marking boundaries

Fences give the garden its main vertical structure. While keeping children and pets in, and intruders out, they also have a significant influence on the design of the space. Depending on the circumstances, garden boundaries can be emphasized or played down – you might want to have an uninterrupted view of beautiful countryside or to obscure an unsightly urban landmark. There is often a contrast between the boundaries around the front and back gardens of a house. At the front, the wall or fence is often low or visually lightweight, marking the boundary without obscuring the view of the house, to provide an open, welcoming appearance. At the back, however, it is more likely to be solid, to give privacy from neighbouring gardens. As well as perimeter walls or fences, you may wish to erect boundaries within the garden, to divide different areas. These often take the form of an open screen that allows you to see through into another part of the garden.

TRELLIS PANELS

Garden fences can be used as a support structure for trellis panels. This rustic trellis adds visual interest as well as making a framework for a montage of climbing roses and decorative features such as twiggy hearts and stars and metal lanterns.

PICKET BOUNDARY

Classic picket fencing is a perennial favourite for cottage front gardens, and always looks good when used along the whole street for continuity. But instead of choosing predictable white, these neighbours have painted their fences in complementary colours to differentiate between the two properties.

DIVIDE THE GARDEN

Creating compartments within a garden helps to engender an illusion of space or emphasize a focal point. In this case, large trellis screens are used to highlight a grotto-style water feature. Trellis panels come in a wide variety of sizes and shapes, and the solid supporting posts can be finished off with architectural finials such as globes or obelisks.

MAKE A TRELLIS SCREEN

This trellis divides off part of the garden without obscuring the view. Painted in soft blue-green, it tones perfectly with garden greens and provides an excellent framework for a climbing rose and a clematis. Paradoxically, introducing screens into even the smallest garden creates an illusion of space because there is a feeling of more going on beyond.

WATER BOUNDARY

A sheet of water provides the ultimate translucent boundary, sectioning off part of the garden without dividing it up visually. Poles painted in watery colours continue the boundary effect through the garden. To create this fabulous shimmering wall, you will need to install a tank fitted with a pump at its foot. The water can then be pumped up the uprights to create the waterfall.

decorative structures

If you have room in your garden it makes sense to add a structural element that will give a focal point, and in many cases real decorative input. Many garden buildings can be bought 'off the shelf' from garden centres or specialist suppliers, ready to assemble on site. These can be customized in whatever way you want, with climbing plants, or hanging decorations. You can also completely change the appearance with paints or wood stains. Bear in mind that dark colours will appear to recede and lighter ones come forward, so the position of your structure should be taken into consideration. You should also choose a colour that adds impact to your planting. You may want to provide contrast to foliage, or perhaps match particular flowers to give them more importance when they appear. Remember, too, that the buildings will look more prominent in winter when the trees are bare and many plants have died down.

FAIRYTALE WIREWORK

The tracery of wire mesh makes a far less dominant structure than traditional wood, bringing architecture to a space without overpowering it. This reproduction Victorian aviary makes a charming garden ornament that can be planted with climbers such as clematis.

ADD COLOUR WITH PAINT

Give your garden all-year colour by painting the garden shed, fencing and pergola in co-ordinating colours. Here, blues and purples tone with summer planting, yet look good all winter long, even when there is little plant cover.

SIZE MATTERS

If you want a large structure, but don't want it to dominate, choose one that will act as a see-through screen, rather than one made of a solid material. This metalwork pergola makes a romantic focal point, appearing to float in the wildflower meadow. And although it is large enough to seat half a dozen people, it enhances, rather than obscures the space it is in.

ARCHITECTURAL INTEREST

Even tiny buildings add structure to the garden. This sentry box structure, just large enough to house a single chair, is an inspired choice for a small patio garden. It is painted a subtle blue-grey to complement the two standard silvery willows (*Salix alba* var. *sericea*) that flank it.

houses and arbours

Garden architecture sounds far too grand for tiny gardens, but if it is well planned, there is room for structure in even the smallest space. Far from having a cluttering effect, it can actually visually expand it, and can certainly make your outdoor space more flexible. A small town garden for example, provides very little play space for children, yet by installing a pretty little playhouse, it can be transformed into a miniature wonderland. And where there is scant room for tables and chairs, a fence-side arbour and seat can provide the starting point for dinner *à deux* outside.

PLAY CORNER

This customized playhouse makes a pretty feature in the corner of a garden, whilst giving the children a fairytale cottage for play. It started life as an off-the-shelf building, and the first step was to enlarge the windows to accommodate the smallest available shutters. Roof slates and ridge tiles replaced roofing felt, and ready-made fretwork was added to the eaves. Finally, the whole structure was painted an attractive colour to tone in well with the dark foliage all around.

THE HOUSE JACK BUILT

If you feel confident enough to build your own structure (or know someone else who can), you can get the children to help design their very own playhouse. This little crooked house, complete with veranda and smiley-face chimney, is built on stilts to provide two storeys of playspace. The children love climbing the short stairway up to the front door into their own no-adults-allowed playspace. It is a truly charming garden feature that should last for generations.

▶ A TRELLIS ARBOUR

Trellis panels can be made up into an arbour for even the smallest garden. This enchanting bower was constructed using lattice trellis then painted with a decorative exterior woodstain to tone with the bench. The whole structure is supported by six 7.5 x 7.5cm/3 x 3in wooden posts, each 2.2m/7ft long. They are set in 7.5 x 7.5cm/3 x 3in metal post holders with 75cm/2½ft long spikes. The back is formed by a 180 x 90cm/6 x 3ft trellis panel. Three 180 x 60cm/6 x 2ft panels are used for the two sides and the roof. Two narrow 180 x 30cm/6 x 1ft panels and a concave 180 x 45cm/6 x 1½ft panel are used for the front.

1 Cut the six wooden posts to length. They should be 180cm/6ft long plus the depth of the metal 'shoe' at the top of the metal spike, which will hold the post.

2 Mark positions for the two back posts 180cm/6ft apart, then, using a mallet, drive in a spiked metal post holder at each position. As you drive it in, check that it is going in straight. Stand a post in each of the holders.

3 Temporarily fix the top of the back panel to the top of the posts, using 5cm/2in galvanized nails and a hammer.

4 Drill pilot holes for the screws at intervals down each side of the trellis, using a No.8 bit. Drill through the trellis into the posts. Fix the panel in position using 3cm/1¼in No.10 zinc-coated steel screws.

5 Set up the two front outside posts as in step 2 and fix the side panels as in steps 3 and 4.

6 Set up the two inside front posts and fix the upright front panels as above. Fix the concave panel between these panels.

7 Place the roof panel in position on top of the posts. Fix it firmly in place, as above, screwing down into the posts.

8 Paint the arbour with exterior woodstain, or, if you prefer, a coat of decorative paint, and leave to dry.

▲ *Most of the time this arbour provides a tranquil place to sit, but with a little imagination it can be transformed for all sorts of occasions. Here, a low table laid with a colourful cloth and candles is set off by garden flares, creating a gypsy campfire feel. Pure white linen and crockery accompanied by tiny candle lanterns would produce a sophisticated look, while bright primary colours, bunches of balloons and bunting would set the scene for a children's tea party.*

watery elements

The addition of a water feature can open up new vistas in the garden. Water provides a mirror-like surface that reflects shimmering light and brings the evocative sound of splashing and trickling. A pond gives new planting opportunities, providing a habitat for aquatic, marginal and bog plants, while enhancing the ecosystem of the entire garden. Water features come in all shapes and sizes, ranging from naturalistic wildlife ponds to highly stylized modern designs that determine the character of the whole garden. Installing a water feature requires some understanding of basic principles, not only of specialized planting, but of pumps and filters, too. If, on the other hand, you are more interested in smaller-scale water projects decide on what it is you want to focus on. You might want the sound of water in your garden, or a watery element to grow a specific kind of plant, or something that will attract birds.

COMBINE DECKING AND A POOL

Incorporate a water feature into the decking, either in the main part of the garden, as here, or even as part of the patio. This isn't a viable choice for families with small children, but for those who don't have to worry so much about the safety aspect, decking and water suit each other very well, and the combination looks modern, simple and smart. Here, clean lines and restrained planting work together to create a tranquil pool area, linking a wooden terrace with the main garden.

BUILD A RAISED POND

You can avoid digging by building above ground level and lining the retaining structure with butyl rubber. This simple raised pond provides a decorative focal point for a walled kitchen garden, while the low-powered jet disturbs the surface of the pool. The slate slab surround doubles up as seating.

BLUE WATER

This formal pool is tiny, but its impact is considerable because of the bright colours. The harlequin design of blue and aquamarine mosaic tiles adds a distinctly Mediterranean feel.

MINI WATER FEATURES

You don't need to have an enormous garden to fit some kind of water element in. A pond in a pot, for example, is a quick and easy to establish. Ordinary water lilies need a lot of space and depth to grow, so choose a miniature variety such as pink *Nymphaea* 'Froebelii', shown here, and white *N. odorata* var. *minor*.

▶ *Wall masks take up little space for a considerable impact. You will still be able to enjoy the gentle plashing sound, and birds will be attracted to the shallow water.*

▼ *Water flows over this exquisite scallop shell before dropping gently into a little deep wall-mounted pool – a truly elegant design. If you need to keep your garden safe for children, consider a bubbling water feature where the water flows over a pile of pebbles and sinks away to an underground tank before being pumped back through the circuit.*

a lick of paint

Let paint or woodstain bring all-year colour to your garden. Choose paint for an opaque effect; woodstain for a more translucent look that allows the grain to show through. Garden furniture can be painted at any time of the year, the very best time being summer, when the paint will dry quickly. Fences, trellis, garden buildings and walls however are best painted on fine days in autumn, winter or early spring, when there is least plant growth to get in the way or be damaged by any paint splashes. As well as bringing permanent colour to the garden, painted surfaces can be used to complement the planting to give it strength. The wall behind a lavender hedge, for example, can be painted to match the silvery foliage, making a strong silvery-green statement in winter, yet setting off the summer blooms.

SHEDWORKS

Even the most unpromising garden buildings can be turned into something special. This garden building started life as little more than a concrete block. With the addition of some decorative plaster shapes and strong paint colour, it took on the appearance of a miniature Mediterranean villa. The paint effects were achieved using a combination of emulsion (latex) paint, artist's acrylic and fine-textured masonry paint and acrylic scumble glaze. The door has been given a Moorish look by the addition of shaped MDF (medium-density fibreboard). The plaster shapes were fixed to the wall using exterior tile adhesive.

1 Draw a Moorish roof motif on a piece of paper to fit the top of the door. Cut out and check the size against the door. Transfer the shape to a piece of MDF and cut out with a jigsaw (saber saw).

2 Prime both the door and the MDF shape with acrylic primer, and leave to dry. Paint them with dark blue emulsion (latex) paint and leave to dry.

3 Mix up a glaze using white fine-textured masonry paint, acrylic scumble glaze and a little water until it is the consistency of double (heavy) cream. Tint with light blue acrylic. Use this to paint the door and the MDF shape, then quickly wipe the glaze with a soft cloth. Allow to dry.

4 Nail the MDF shape to the door and touch up the nail heads with some of the pale blue glaze.

5 Using a stiff brush, scrub the wall surfaces to remove the dirt. Fix the plaster shapes to the wall using exterior tile adhesive. Secure them temporarily in position with electrical tape while the adhesive dries.

6 Prime and paint the wall including the shapes with white fine-textured masonry paint. Allow to dry thoroughly.

7 Tint three pots of acrylic scumble with acrylic paint – one red, one orange, one yellow. Using a damp sponge, wipe the colours randomly on the wall, blending the edges. Wipe off the excess with a cloth.

8 Using an artist's brush, stipple extra colour into any detailing for emphasis. Leave to dry for at least four hours, then coat with polyurethane varnish.

COLOUR WITH STRIPES

A decorative edge in stripes of bright Caribbean colours gives life to a plain white wall and door. Masking tape was used to keep the lines straight. When they were all complete and dry, the leaves were stencilled in position to add extra interest. Quick and easy to do, the colours are easily changed whenever you're ready for a new look.

ATTRACTING THE LIGHT

Use colour and reflections to bring light and a feeling of space into a tiny courtyard. Here, pale yellow walls and sand-coloured gravel lend a light feel, which is further magnified by the 'cascade' of a mirror mosaic bouncing sunlight back into the space.

MEDITERRANEAN EFFECTS

Faded plaster walls and sun-bleached shutters provide a strong backdrop that sets the ambience in this delightful Mediterranean courtyard garden.

NATURAL ELEGANCE

Garden furniture doesn't necessarily have to be painted in the brightest of colours to create an interesting effect. Taupe and white make an elegant combination for a simple slatted folding chair. The use of these unassuming colours brings Italian-style flair to a garden that is already rich in the soft natural tones of weathered wood. Baskets, casually left lying around after use, make attractive occasional features, but as soon as rain threatens they will need to be returned to a shed or summerhouse for protection.

arches and climbers

You need a serious amount of space for an arched walkway, but if you do have the room they make wonderful year-round garden decorations. In the growing season the mass of plants that climb around them hide the arch completely, creating a lovely visual illusion of plant architecture, and in the winter months when the plants die back the curves and points of the arch itself become visible, giving the garden much needed interest and decoration. But the most glorious element of all arches is the planting: wonderful climbers, trained over the years to scramble up and over. You can create this effect on a much smaller scale by training plants to climb up wigwams, obelisks, miniature willow ornaments or a wall trellis. Positioned carefully, these planting arrangements will add height and interest to any garden.

◄ A METAL WALKWAY
Install a support that looks beautiful in its own right, however long the plants take to grow up it. This pagoda-topped walkway lends an almost oriental feel to the garden. Beautiful, old Greek *pithoi*, in muted terracotta tones that echo the paving bricks, are used to great effect as the focal point at the end of the path.

◄ A GOLDEN ARCH
Cascades of laburnum make a flamboyant golden archway in the summertime. To create the effect, two rows of trees were grown up and over a metal walkway.

PRETTY AND PRACTICAL

Grow vibrant scarlet runner beans up a wigwam of canes to bring height and colour to the vegetable garden or produce to the flower beds. This is not only attractive, but produces a considerable crop during late summer.

CLEMATIS OBELISK

You can train tangle-prone clematis up a sturdy support in a border to concentrate the blooms and create a more colourful effect. This tall wooden obelisk is the right scale for a large country garden.

ROSES ALL THE WAY

A rose arch is the epitome of the cottage garden style – and for good reason. As well as supporting a delightful froth of blooms, even better if they are scented, the arch creates a simple screening effect that gives an illusion of space.

FLOWERS AND FRUIT

This beautiful old stone balustrade, partly covered by climbing roses and vines, gives a tantalizing glimpse of the garden beyond. As the rose blooms die down, juicy bunches of grapes dangling from the intertwining vines begin to mature.

plants in training

Trimmed, clipped, trained or shaped, there are many reasons for coaxing plants into different forms. Much loved in the eighteenth century, topiary shapes bring soft architectural form to the garden, which is still popular in both traditional and modern gardens today. Clipping plants also helps to keep them under control. For example, enthusiastic herbs such as rosemary, sage and bay can be kept in shape so they can fit into even the smallest kitchen garden. Clipped and standardized plants can be planted straight into the ground. Alternatively, they can go into containers to provide extra flexibility, as they then can be moved around the garden according to the season, bringing colour where it is most needed at the time.

FLOWERING STANDARDS

It's possible to standardize many flowering shrubs, such as this hydrangea, to make delightful ornamental trees. Once the shrub is mature enough to show a main stem, prune off the lower branches to encourage the top ones to flourish. You will have to prune back the lower shoots regularly, as a healthy hydrangea will be inclined to keep producing them around ground level. Planted in containers, flowering standards can be moved into focal positions while they are blooming.

SANTOLINA TOPIARY

Standardize a santolina to keep it under control. The pretty grey leaves and yellow flowers of santolina make it a desirable all-year plant – but it spreads prolifically. If your garden is small, the ideal solution is to keep it in a pot and either standardize it like this, or trim it into a dome or cone.

ESPALIER FRUIT TREES

A favourite in the kitchen gardens of large country houses, espaliered fruit trees might seem a little grand for the average city plot. However, as well as posessing great charm, they are highly practical. Trained against the wall, they provide structure, take up little space, and yet can produce a healthy crop of fruit. This young apple tree was bought in a pot, already trained into the espalier habit. It will continue to grow happily in a large pot, but needs seasonal attention with the secateurs to keep it neat and tidy against the wall. The ballerina cherry trees on either side of it, with their brilliant pink flowers, bring out the delicate blush-pink of the apple blossom. These remarkable looking plants are deliberately bred to grow in their characteristic pole-like fashion and don't require any hard pruning, unlike the espalier.

SMALL-SCALE TOPIARY

Mini topiaries look great on a patio, providing architectural form on a scale that relates to the space. These box topiaries (home-made or ready-made) need to be clipped only once a year, in early summer. The miniature cone and ball make useful focal points in a small patio garden. Topiary can be bought ready shaped, but if you have patience you can grow your own, using either your eye or a chickenwire form to create a simple shape.

THEATRICAL STYLE

Small triple-crown box balls, planted in oversized ornamental terracotta pots, make a witty, theatrical statement. They give the impression of coming from Alice's Wonderland, where her size and that of her everyday surroundings had a habit of changing and distorting proportions. Despite the stage-style nature of the planting, when they are mulched with large white pebbles, the topiaries retain an elegance befitting a formal Italianate garden. The large containers lend them prominence while they are still young, but allow for plenty of future growing space. Cutting and training a feature plant such as this requires some skill and is best left to expert hands.

potted plants

Put colour and structure in your garden exactly where you want it by planting up containers. Planters teamed with the right plants have an architectural quality and lend style and focus to the garden. But the main advantage of containers is that you can move them to a prominent part of the garden while their contents are at their best, then hide them in the 'nursery' while they are going through their resting periods. This is most useful when growing spring bulbs: they arrive with a showy display of colour and demand to be put centre stage, but when the flowers are over, their wilting leaves need time to soak up the sun. In a container, they can do this out of sight while alternative pots of early summer flowers take their place.

PERFECT PROPORTIONS

The key to clever planting lies in achieving a balance between the plant and the pot, but confusingly there are few rules. The only real rule you have to follow is to make sure the earth is covered – either by the main plant and its own leaves, by an underplanting, or by attractive mulching. For the latter, almost anything will work – pretty pebbles, chopped bark, glass nuggets, shells, slate chippings, or even corks. Make sure the plants neither look too big for the pot, nor too insignificant, matching chunky plants with chunky pots and grouping them to make a pleasing balanced display. This smart modern planting was inspired by a trio of architectural zinc containers. Tightly packed *Sempervivum* (houseleeks) make a neat topping for a tall round pot, and is complemented by a smaller 'cousin' in the background. The third, square-sided pot has been planted with a wilder-looking ornamental grass for contrast.

◀ *A large pot with a thyme collection arranged around a sundial creates a visual pun. Thymes come in many varieties, with leaves that range from yellow to blue-green and with pretty lilac, purple or palest pink flowers, depending on the variety, and they always look good together. Plant them next to contrasting neighbours for definition. Thyme can spread very enthusiastically in the summer, so if you need to keep them under control, for example to keep this sundial on view, you will have to prune them regularly for the cooking pot. Thyme is evergreen and either fully hardy or half hardy, depending on the type, so keep plants in a sheltered spot if you want them to survive the winter.*

MATCH PLANTS TO POTS

Scale is important. This tiny viola has been potted up in an equally tiny zinc container to show off the delicate detail of the flowers. In a larger container, with a mass of flowers, the effect would just be a blur.

▲ *Show off lily-of-the-valley in matching white-painted pots. The fragrant flowers are much too gorgeous to be left hidden away in a border, so lift some plants and pot them up to enjoy them where you can see and smell them best.*

POTS OF BLOSSOM

In spring, when blossom adorns the trees and bulbs hug the ground, there can be a lack of colour in between. Tuck blossoms into tiny glass jars and hang them at eye level, near the patio perhaps.

PRETTY POTS

Spruce up plain terracotta pots, then plant them with springtime favourites. These pots have been decorated with a simple mosaic pattern, using colourful ceramic fragments. Cover the back of each fragment with tile adhesive, press on to the pot, and fill the gaps with coloured grout.

▼ *A necklace made of sea-smoothed glass collected from the beach turns a pot of lettuce into something special.*

creative containers

Sometimes it is the containers themselves, rather than the plants, that provide the main interest, bringing colour or wit to the planting. Look out for interesting functional containers in beautiful colours, such as enamelware or old kitchen tableware, or paint up some pots in vibrant colours that will look fabulous in the garden all year round. Trawl junk shops for wonderful old metalware, or paint some metallic effects on to inexpensive new items. The plantings in these can be changed as the seasons pass for all-year interest and colour. Some containers are designed as sculptures in themselves, and often require particular types of plant to set them off. If this is the case, choose evergreens, which will look good all year round.

POT HEAD
This garden container is a sculpture in itself, and, with the addition of a flamboyant golden grass, the head is given a witty punky hairdo.

KITCHEN CAST OFFS
Large food cans are often decorated with attractive graphics and it can seem a waste to discard them after their contents have been consumed. Give them new life as colourful containers for small plants, perhaps grouping them together on a board or low wall. Make drainage holes by hammering a nail through the bottom before planting them up.

MEXICAN-STYLE POTS
These bright, seemingly intricate designs are deceptively easy to do. Use masking tape to mask off the pots in bands, and paint stripes of lively colours between the tapes. When the paint has dried, peel off the masking tape to reveal stripes of colour and bare terracotta. Paint simple motifs on each band in white for a look that brings all-year colour to the garden.

EYE-LEVEL COLOUR

A wooden container on a post, topped with a humorous wooden bird, is planted with jolly blue forget-me-nots to bring colour up to eye level where it is most needed in spring.

PAINTED POTS

If you can't find the genuine article, give a cheap aluminium bucket the patina of old copper with an easily applied paint effect. Prime with metal primer, then paint with gold then amber shellac. For the verdigris effect, sponge on a dilute mix of aqua and white acrylic paint. When dry, protect with coats of polyurethane varnish.

TEA POTS

Recycle old teapots, mugs and jugs from junk shops, as colourful containers. Drill drainage holes, then plant them up with flowering plants in co-ordinating tones to make a delightful montage.

▲ *Another way to distribute colour at eye level is to plant brightly coloured flowers in hanging containers. Receptacles of all kinds can be transformed into 'hanging baskets', and they may turn up in the most unlikely places. This copper builder's bucket was bought in a French flea market.*

unusual ornaments

Decorative details help to express your personality in the garden. You may not be in the market for expensive sculpture, but anything you add in addition to the plants can reinforce the style and structure of your outdoor space: painted pots, unusual plant supports, bird baths, bird houses, even plant labels and piles of stones. Anything that is weatherproof can be used ornamentally outside, just as it would be inside your home. Arrange shells on a patio side table, make a wirework and raffia heart to hang in a tree, let old watering cans become sculptures in themselves. Root around junk shops and architectural salvage yards and seek out beautiful old metal drain covers or pieces of elaborate metalwork, which can become plant supports whilst providing visual interest in the flower borders all year long.

LOOKING FOR THE UNUSUAL
The cost of garden statuary is prohibitive for many of us, and in a small scale garden, it is in danger of looking out of place. One solution is to hunt out interesting pieces in junk shops or to concoct your own 'sculptures' from found objects. Almost anything that adds structure to the garden can be used, whether it is something that started out large, or something you 'build', such as a pile of pebbles. This old wicker mannequin makes a witty and unexpected life-size garden ornament. A miniature wire version has been set against it to make a play on size. The potted clematis nearby will soon colonize the mannequin and if not kept in check could hide the wicker from view.

▼ *Hanging from a tree, a Victorian metal bird cage makes a pretty garden ornament. Instead of a live creature, it is now home to a little pot of flowers.*

WHITHER THE WILLOWS

Willow has been used for hundreds of years as a traditional English fencing material, and so has proved it will survive outside in and in summer and winter. In recent years, it has become popular as a sculpting material, and can be made up into wonderful witty, life-size farm animals that don't look out of place in even the smallest of gardens. These willow sculptures aren't too difficult to find in country areas where they are made; but why not try to make one yourself? You will need to do it in spring, when the withies (willow twigs) are still green and flexible. Start by making a chickenwire base, add four stout branches for legs, then weave in the soaked withies to build up the shape.

GARDEN SHED SCARECROW

A scarecrow sculpture can usually be made from garden shed items and unwanted old clothes. This dapper chap has hand-tool hands and a colander face. He wears an old denim jacket and sporty panama hat. You can change his outfit and attitude regularly during the summer to keep the interest going.

STONE SCULPTURE

Pile up some flat stones pagoda-style for an easy sculpture with an eastern influence. This is a miniature attempt, but if you collect large flat stones, you will be surprised at how high you can build whilst retaining sufficient stability.

fixed furniture

Furnishing the garden turns it into an inviting place to relax, eat and entertain. Grand traditional gardens were often furnished with permanent fixtures, such as stone benches, which became as much a part of the garden architecture as small buildings and gazebos. Furniture that is either too heavy to move or is fixed still contributes to the garden's architecture, though nowadays there is a greater variety in materials, scale and design. Made from stone, wood, metal or a combination of these, it can be both a focal point and, in small gardens, a space-saving device.

A FITTING PLACE

Built-in furniture makes the best use of tiny spaces outdoors, just as it does inside. This tight corner would have been wasted space without this cleverly designed unit. The round table is wrapped around by a low bench, which transforms the corner into a delightful outdoor dining area with room for at least three around the table plus more along the benches. The aromatic herbs incorporated into the table provide a charming touch.

SCULPTURE TO SIT ON

Invest in functional sculpture. This stunning carved bench, with its curved interlocking form, has an exquisite shape that would elevate any garden setting. But it is more than sculpture – it is also a practical bench that is very much used.

SITTING PRETTY

Cast iron and timber slatted benches might not be actually fixed in position, but they are far too heavy to move around on a regular basis, and so need to be given a permanent position within the garden. This bench has been brought right up to date with a coat of soft grey-blue paint that brings all-year colour to a peaceful corner of the garden.

SLEEK STYLE

This chunky modern metal bench provides a solid structural element to one side of a small city patio. It could not be simpler, but, when teamed with neatly clipped and potted evergreens and matched by a similar ensemble on the other side of the patio, it is undeniably smart and makes a welcoming spot for sitting outside on a hot summer's day.

ON THE TABLE

Before you throw out unwanted furniture from inside the house, consider whether it could be used in the garden. This console table, set against a wall, and subtly decorated with stencilled leaves, is perfect for displaying blooming plants. It also doubles up as a useful work surface for quick garden tasks such as potting on seedlings or planting up spring bulbs.

garden relaxation

Your garden furniture needs to suit your garden, and doesn't necessarily have to be based on large gatherings around a huge table. Consider how you might use your outside living spaces; perhaps a couple of smaller, flexible seating arrangements would work better for you. A couple of chairs and a small table for each of them, or folding chairs that you can move at will, or a few wooden benches dotted around a large garden will give you greater adaptability. Most verandahs can accommodate at least two chairs; on the tiniest patio, you can usually also add a low side table. So think of all of the outdoor parts of your home as extra living space: bring out the furniture on sunny days and balmy nights to enjoy relaxing times with family and friends or a little well-earned peace and quiet. If you have a large garden, your place for relaxation doesn't have to be next to the house – why not create a patio area in a secluded corner of the garden, to make an outdoor room that can be a wonderful quiet retreat.

TAKE YOUR SEATS

Where the garden is too small for permanent seating, take comfortable chairs into the garden exactly where you want to relax – in or out of the sun. Folding canvas chairs can be placed on the smallest patio to create an instant garden idyll. These smart umbrella-fold canvas chairs are neat to store, easy to move and yet are incredibly comfortable. Here, they nestle next to a garden stream surrounded by shrubs and perennials.

TEMPORARY LUXURY

If you are making an effort for a special day in the garden, consider doing some serious furniture removals and transport a little section of your living room outside. If you are certain of the weather and have the time to indulge yourself, what could be more enjoyable than being this comfortable in your own garden? Wicker chairs like these are ideal as they are not too heavy, and yet are as comfortable as any upholstered piece.

ROSY BOWER

Group furniture in private corners. This outdoor living room, sheltered by swathes of roses growing on trellis, makes a beautiful secluded spot that is protected from the wind.

PATIO COLOUR

Paint the simplest garden bench, add some colourful cushions and you have an attractive outdoor sofa. An occasional table turns this little corner of the patio into a summer outdoor living room.

WATERPROOF STYLE

Bring the indoors out by re-upholstering an old chair in plasticized cloth. This inexpensive Louis XIV-style chair, painted in pale green and upholstered in flowery PVC (vinyl), makes a witty statement.

tables and table dressing

In summer, a little extra exterior design can do as much for the garden as interior design can indoors. Stamp your personality on to your outdoor space by bringing out some occasional furniture and furnishings, and dressing them up or down to suit the occasion. An extra table or two can be very useful, providing surfaces for decorative touches, such as potted plants or garden ornaments, as well as for serving summer food and drinks. Fold up tables are particularly useful as they can spend most of their time in the shed protected from the elements, yet be easily brought out when needed. Throw over a colourful cloth to completely transform the table, then lay it for a lunch party on a sunny summer's day. Indoor-outdoor tables with weatherproof surfaces, such as mosaic or glass that will survive a surprise shower, are also ideal as occasional outdoor furnishings.

MAKING A MOSAIC TABLE TOP

Creating your own mosaic can be extremely satisfying and is not hard to do. You need a clean, plain table top and plenty of unwanted or broken glazed tiles and china in suitable colours. Before you begin, cut the pieces to size, using tile nippers.

1 Draw the design on the table top, using a pencil, then paint the whole surface with wood primer.

2 'Butter' tile adhesive on to the back of a mosaic piece, and fix it in position. When you have completed the mosaic, leave it to dry.

3 Wearing plastic gloves, work tile grout between the tiles, using your fingers then a dishwashing brush. Clean off any excess with a sponge.

GARDEN MOSAICS

Both weatherproof and highly decorative, mosaic makes a great outdoor surface. It looks fantastic just as it is, providing a colourful, wipe-clean surface with no need for a tablecloth, even if you are using it for outdoor eating. A table top provides the perfect flat surface for mosaic work, giving you plenty of space to develop an attractive design that will make a delightful summer focal point. This mosaic has been made from bits of broken old china pots and chipped decorative tiles. Make sure you have enough materials to finish the design before you begin.

▶ *A more formal design such as this is probably good to begin with if you haven't done a mosaic before. The geometric pattern makes it a quick and easy design to follow. The different blues and greens complement each other perfectly.*

DRESSING UP

If you are spending long summer days in the garden, you might like to dress your table up by covering it with a cloth. It doesn't have to be for a special occasion or even a meal, but rather to add colour and movement to your outside room. You don't need to expose your best linen to the elements, either. Use lengths of cheap fabric or even plastic-coated paper so that you can throw it away when you want a change or if it has rained too many times. Make a splash in a corner of a springtime garden, as here, by covering any old wooden table (or even a pile of boxes) with a colourful checked cloth, then 'laying' it with co-ordinated painted pots that are planted with daffodils. This is an ideal way to introduce colour at eye level at a time of the year when garden interest tends to be limited to low-growing bulbs or blossoms high up on boughs. Later in the year you can display cut flowers in this way.

◀ *A joyous striped cloth, teamed with prettily painted enamelware, makes a special treat of tea-time in the garden. A pitcher crammed with jolly flowers adds the finishing touch that brings indoor style out into the garden.*

▼ *In sheltered spots and summer houses, outdoor decoration can be every bit as subtle as indoors, and you don't even have to use your best linen. Here, an old sheet, given a decorative hem of twigs and chains, makes a charming statement.*

windowsill art

Windowsills are important because they act as a link between house and garden and work both ways, from outside as well as indoors. They can be decorated much the same way as a mantelpiece in a living room can be, with traditional window boxes or other smaller containers of any kind to make a pleasing arrangement. Just like any other containers, window boxes allow you to create a moveable garden that can be switched as the seasons progress, adding colour to the view from inside the house and embellishment to the outside.

TERRACOTTA LINE UP

A line of tiny pots, each planted with a different auricula, brings springtime colour to a window sill. The wonderful colours and immaculate detail of auriculas engaged Victorian enthusiasts so much that they constructed special 'theatres' in which to display them while in bloom. On the windowsill, the flowers can still take centre stage. It is best to stand pots on some kind of tray to protect the paintwork, which would quickly become damaged by permanently standing pot bases.

A SHELL WINDOW BOX

Decorate a window box with a pattern of mussel shells, then plant it up with colour-co-ordinating lavender and violas for an all-summer display. The subtle colour gradation of the violas makes them a perfect match for the pearly interiors of the shells, which in turn are surprisingly robust and weatherproof.

WINDOW BOX TOPIARY

A collection of evergreens makes a sculptural all-year display. The basic structure of this planting is formed by a central box pyramid flanked by two box balls. White bacopa is added in front in the spring, and can be replaced by seasonal bedding plants as the year progresses.

A WINDOWSILL GARDEN

This long-lasting display contains tiny spring-flowering violas and summer-flowering convolvulus, bacopa, petunias and lavender in co-ordinating colours, against a background of silvery helichrysum.

PURE WHITE AND GREEN

Showy white pelargoniums are the centrepiece of this smart arrangement, flanked by pretty marguerite daisies and tiny white bacopa. The grey foliage is senecio. White plantings like this are always effective, and as the seasons change, new white blooms can replace the old.

THRESHOLD COLOUR

Potted red geraniums placed on a tiny balcony provide a perfect visual link between a sparsely decorated house and this lovely garden crammed full of plants.

sound in the garden

Every garden has its own natural sounds that change and evolve through the seasons. The first cuckoo call is traditionally seen as the herald of spring, but is now somewhat rare. We are more likely to hear the comforting coo of woodpigeons or doves. But even in the city, the sweet birdsong of spring builds up to a crescendo as summer approaches, then bees and other insects join the orchestra, filling the air with the hum of busy wings. Wind rustles the leaves and branches of trees and shrubs. You can add more 'natural' sound to the garden: hang up windchimes (you can make your own) to make music in the breeze, or introduce a water feature, however small, to your own private plot so that water splashes and trickles all day long.

NATURAL MUSIC

Sand dollars, shells and raffia can be made up into unusual windchimes that are bold enough to make a striking ornament while bringing a distinctive sound to the garden. They are incredibly quick and easy to make because sand dollars naturally feature a hole, which comes in very handy for threading raffia. A sand dollar is the skeleton of a sea animal with a five-part symmetrical body – starfish and sea urchins are part of the same group, but sand dollars are any of the flattened varieties. They're found in the shallow waters off the North American coast. They can be bought in some gift, craft and bathroom shops. Beware collecting them yourself. In many areas it is an offence to take shells out of the country and certainly it is an illegal to harm any living animals for their shells. A 'fringe' of cockle shells, hung below the sand dollar trio, are what make the music.

1 Start by drilling a hole through the bottom of ten cockle shells. Tie one shell to each end of three lengths of raffia about 60cm/2ft long and to each end of two lengths of raffia about 45cm/18in long.

2 Fold all five lengths in half and gather them together at the halfway point. Thread this loop through the hole in one sand dollar. Feed the ends of the raffia, including shells, through the loop and pull tight.

3 Take two further lengths of raffia and feed them through the same hole in the sand dollar, then tie the ends at the top of the sand dollar. In the same way, tie on two other sand dollars to make the top of the chime.

NOISY SCULPTURE

While small chimes tinkle with the slightest breeze, large ones make deep mellow sounds that can be reassuringly comforting. This outsized sculptural windchime creates a melodious and peaceful ambience in the garden. Made from narrow slivers of silvery slate, it also changes, chameleon-like, with the weather, becoming shiny black when it is damp or wet, and dusty-pale when dry.

A GENTLE TRICKLE

Even if you don't have the space or inclination to install a full-blown water feature in your garden, you need not be deprived of the evocative sound of trickling water. For example, water bubbling from the mouth of this ceramic pot into a large bowl of pebbles makes a gentle murmur that enhances a summer's day. It only requires a small pump at the bottom of the bowl to keep the water moving.

TINKLING TONES

Water trickling against metal makes a gentle, persistent sound in this futuristic garden feature.

RECYCLED SOUND

A visit to the garden shed and a drinks party are all that you need to construct these rustic windchimes. The 'bells' are made from miniature terracotta garden pots with metal vine eyes as clappers.

THE SWEETEST SOUNDS

Windchimes combine sweet sound with style. Some are beautifully tuned by their makers, so that no matter what order the tubes are struck as they move about in the wind, the music is always pleasing to the ear. Test as many different kinds as you can before making your selection.

hanging decorations

Decorations that dangle are extremely useful for bringing year-round interest into the garden, brightening walls, enhancing bare branches and generally taking on the job that pictures occupy inside the house. Almost any material can be used for an outdoor hanging as long as it is weatherproof: garden wire, chickenwire, raffia, china, reflective glass and mirror, painted or stained wood, twigs, branches, pine cones and anything organic. Generally, you need to think big in the garden – even a small 10m/30ft plot is large compared to the average living room, so most decorations need to be visible from some distance. For the same reason, simple shapes work best, as they need to stand out clearly against the foliage.

PRACTICAL SOLUTION

If a good long hot spell is forecast, you can dry garden-grown chillies outdoors, threading them on to wooden skewers, then chaining them up for a decorative display. They will make a fabulous, colourful temporary show, and once dried they can be stored in airtight jars for months, ready for tasty winter dishes. If rain threatens while the chillies are still drying, whip the whole hanging indoors to continue drying in a well-ventilated room. If they get wet or damp before the drying process is complete, they will be vulnerable to mildew and rot.

HEARTS IN THE GARDEN

Hearts hold universal appeal, and their wonderful simple outline works well in the garden. This delightful filigree heart is easy to make from garden wire, and it is certainly robust enough to withstand a winter outside. It is composed of several smaller hearts, bent to shape using household pliers, wired together to make a beautiful all-over design. Make just one and hang it in a tree. Alternatively, make several in different sizes, or even from different types of wire, then group them together on a wall or fence for a delightful display.

FISHING FOR INSPIRATION

Traditional fishermen's floats in coloured glass can make attractive weatherproof garden decorations, especially when they are contained in their original string nets. Hung on garden fence or trellis, they will introduce a quayside appeal.

DECORATIVE TREATS

Hung on chains or ropes to provide winter feasts, treats for garden birds can become decorative features. The birds themselves will add an element of performance art, providing hours of entertainment, and you never know who might drop in.

GARDEN TREASURES

These colourful hearts are decorated with pieces of weathered green bottle glass that were dug up from the garden. Most plots belonging to older houses produce endless fragments of broken china and glass bottles, which can be put to good use like this instead of being thrown away. There is something satisfyingly appealing about turning a previous occupant's discarded rubbish into something beautiful to decorate the garden. The hearts were formed from tile cement, using heart-shaped cookie cutters. A wire loop for hanging was inserted into the top and the glass pressed on before the cement dried. Obviously, you can use this simple technique to produce any other shapes in your cutter collection.

naturally decorative

For garden decorations, you need not look any further than the garden itself. There are plenty of leftovers from seasonal harvests to be gleaned and turned into something beautiful that you can hang on walls, fences, doors and gates. Even if harvest sounds a little grand for your modest plot, you will be surprised by what you can gather. Rose-bush prunings, complete with rosehips, twigs, birds' feathers, lavender blooms, allium heads, and even grass flowerheads, can all be transformed into appealing decorations that will naturally complement the garden, prolonging a season or filling seasonal gaps. You will, of course, need some additional bought materials to effect the transformations, such as raffia and garden wire, but the simpler you keep the decorations, the more natural and exquisite they will look.

WILD BARLEY RING

Wild barley has a wonderful green sheen in midsummer before it begins to ripen and turn yellow. It is not difficult to find in any patch of long grass on common land in early spring. You don't even have to be in the country – the barley used for this wreath was found in a city, growing around trees where the grass had been left unmown. It was in such abundance, even after this bundle had been collected, it was impossible to see where it had been picked. To make the wreath, you will need about 2.4m/8ft of garden wire. Wind this round several times to make a circle approximately 18cm/7in in diameter, and then bind around this with florist's tape. Cut the barley stalks down to 5cm/2in, then bind into bundles of six using the florist's tape. Finally, bind these bundles around the ring using the tape.

SAGE AND TANSY HEART

Like many other herbs, tansy and sage both dry well and they make perfect companions. When picked at its prime, tansy will dry maintaining the yellow colouring of the flowers. For this heart a shape is formed out of thick garden wire and small bunches of the herbs, held together with fine florist's wire, are wired in place to make a charming and aromatic decorative hanging. To hang the heart up, use thick yellow cord that matches the tansy.

WILLOW AND FEATHER STAR

The natural tones of willow sticks and wild bird feathers harmonize beautifully and can very easily be transformed into endless wreaths and hangings. Light and airy in appearance, this delicate-looking star is much more robust than it appears and, fixed firmly into position, can withstand outdoor life. The willow sticks were bound together using raffia and the feathers were stuck on using high-tack glue and then raffia binding.

DOGWOOD HEART

In early spring, the young burgundy-coloured shoots of dogwood are particularly prominent, before the foliage emerges to cover them up. Mature shrubs produce a mass of branches, a few of which can easily be pruned without affecting the overall shape. Use the branches as soon as you can after cutting, while they are still full of sap and pliable. Bend two bundles of twigs into U-shapes, and then put these together to form a heart. Wire all the joints firmly using florist's wire, to stop them from springing back into their original straight position. Then bind the joints with decorative raffia. The result is a delightfully simple red heart that makes a charming outdoor decoration. Some garden dogwoods have twigs in green or black, which can also be used to make decorative hearts.

feathered friends

Birds bring joy to the garden with their birdsong, airborne acrobatics, extrovert courtships and the rearing of their young. They also bring many benefits to the garden, contributing to the ecological balance. Birds will keep insects and other pests under control. Welcome them into the garden with winter food treats and bird baths for a cooling summer splash or to quench their winter thirst when icy ground makes finding water difficult. Offer them nesting boxes to encourage breeding, then watch as they teach their young the rudiments of flight. Many of the facilities you offer can also bring an element of decoration to the garden. Bird boxes can come in as many styles as there is architecture, and they can be painted in colours to co-ordinate with the garden. Bird baths can be constructed from a variety of decorative materials, ranging from traditional stone to colourful mosaic, copper or smooth ceramic.

BIRD ABODES

Line up a street of bird boxes and paint them in bright seaside colours for your own mini beach hut scene. Give the esplanade a miniature picket fence for a smart finishing touch.

◄ *Bird houses hung in trees lend interest in winter, when branches are bare, while keeping their residents relatively safe from cats, especially if hung from a long chain.*

► *Add architectural style with a bird house. This dovecot is made in the form of a fairytale-style European medieval round tower, complete with a curly tiled, steeply pitched roof. The distressed limewash effect gives it an authentic look.*

BATHS AND TABLES

Cover a dish with mosaic to use as a bird bath and garden ornament. This pattern in brown, amber and yellow is made from old broken plates.

▶ *This wigwam-style bird table made from willow twigs is ideal for smaller birds. Bound with raffia, it is robust enough to last the winter. The base is made of 32 willow twigs, woven at either end with raffia, then reinforced on each side with crossways sticks. It is bound at each corner to bundles of twigs, which cross over where the table is tied up.*

▼ *A beaten copper plate hung in the trees makes an exquisite bird bath.*

eating outside

One of the joys of having your own garden is eating outside on a sunny day. There is room to eat even in the smallest plot. Indeed, patio gardens that are paved and planted, rather than lawned, can be the very best eating areas as they are not too far from the house and kitchen. Larger gardens can have an eating area on the deck or patio area, which can be built as a focal point further down the garden. Once your eating area is established, dress it up with cloths, brightly-coloured crockery and quick-and-easy tablecentres to create the impression of an outside room.

MEDITERRANEAN STYLE

The bright colours and vibrant food of the Mediterranean region work well on a summer's day, even in colder climes. This brightly printed Provençal fabric from the south of France provides the perfect backcloth for a setting of simple grilled meat and fish, delicious salads and fresh fruits that are so typical of the region. An array of cheerfully coloured dishes always makes Mediterranean food taste better, even more so when it is liberally sprinkled with health-giving olive oil, which brings out the full flavours.

ENGLISH CREAM TEAS

Freshly baked scones spread with plenty of clotted cream and home-made jam are a favourite English West Country tea-time treat that seems all the more delicious for being enjoyed outdoors. All you need to complete this *al fresco* delight are some wonderful-tasting raspberries picked straight from the garden and a pot of freshly brewed tea. Bring out a small metal table to serve as a tea tray, spread a rug on the lawn, then sit down together to enjoy this special time of day in relaxed and convivial conversation.

LUNCH ON THE LAWN

Lunch taken outside in the summer can be a memorable occasion. Freshly picked garden fruit and salad look wonderful set out on colourful china. Outdoor cooking with family and friends are wonderful opportunities for relaxed fun. Prepare as much as possible in advance.

PICK AND EAT

At a Chinese-style barbecue, garden vegetables are plucked from the ground, prepared outside and put straight into the outdoor wok.

▼ *This delightfully simple meal is made from freshly-picked lettuce leaves, herbs, tomatoes and berries from the garden.*

outdoor table centres

Outdoor table decorations are the very easiest to put together because they are at their most successful when they complement their surroundings. So plunder the garden, then combine the ingredients with flair. You may cut a few flowers, add foliage or even fruit and vegetables; or you may simply gather together some of the smaller pots from around the garden. Make some arrangements for a side table as incidental decoration, or make centrepieces as focal points on *al fresco* buffet tables. A few branches in a tall container or a gathering of potted plants within a wire basket are effective and very quick to do. The secret of success is to concentrate those blooms that grow naturally in looser arrangements throughout the garden in a container on a table.

STRAWBERRY CENTRE

In summer, a couple of potted strawberry plants are transformed into a colourful centrepiece when they are contained within a wire container, then accessorized with a few ripe fruits. Any other shape of wire container would work as well.

ROSY CHARMS

For an enchanting, perfumed garden arrangement, cut the fullest open roses you can find in the garden and place them together in the prettiest china jug. The charm of this arrangement is due to the gathering together of different roses, with no colour co-ordination whatsoever. When garden colours are combined like this, they always seem to work. The gently falling petals add to the effect.

HERBAL HIGHLIGHT

A herbal terracotta centrepiece brings a wonderful aromatic, wild-looking feel to the table. Here, potted lavender, rosemary and thyme are grouped in a large bowl with a golden marigold companion to create a mini apothecary's garden. Handy for use in the kitchen, these potted herbs also perform duty as an informal arrangement wafting pleasing aromas at anyone who casually spends time at the table – preparing vegetables, reading or even doing some homework.

YELLOWS AND BLUE

The sunny yellow faces of sneezeweed become almost luminous when set against the electric blue of 'Blue Butterfly' delphinium. Arranged in a jug with golden-variegated leaves, they bring a wonderful informal summery feel to the table.

garden lighting

Don't let nightfall bring a curfew on enjoying your garden. This is the time when many blooms take on a different, almost luminous quality and perfumes intensify to encourage night-flying insects. Sitting outside for drinks at dusk can be one of the most romantic and evocative times of the day. However, enjoying the garden after nightfall is dependent on lighting, and, in northern climes, heating too, but in many gardens these are sadly lacking. Most permanent outdoor lighting needs to be installed by a professional electrician, who can help you achieve an almost fairytale feel for the garden by enhancing it with pools of light and highlighting focal points. If you are unable to go down that route, however, for special celebrations, you can always add strings of outdoor lights. And for dining after dark, lanterns, patio torches and flares are all useful.

LIGHTING CONSIDERATIONS

Garden lighting serves three purposes. It needs to be functional: lighting the pathway to help you find your way or water features to avoid accidents. It needs to provide security against intruders, and may incorporate movement-sensitive fittings. Finally, it needs to be decorative, and – if you are adventurous – dramatic. It helps to buy all the fittings from one supplier as that will ensure compatibility of both fittings and transformers. Handling electricity is always a specialist job, and, unless you really know what you are doing, don't attempt anything more than plugging in temporary outdoor lighting. If you are having your garden landscaped, you may consider having cables laid and bringing in an expert to work out proper plans. These usually include general lighting for pathways and outdoor buildings, security lighting and spotlighting for focal points. If you don't want the expense of a full outdoor circuit, one of the easiest solutions is to have a powerful outdoor halogen light wired to your indoor circuit to light the patio and shine out into the garden. You can also ask an electrician to fit an all-weather socket outside the house, off the ring main and using this for plugging in temporary lighting. In colder climates, this outdoor socket can be used for patio heaters, which are increasingly available.

POOLS OF LIGHT

Lamps fixed to the building either side of the back door and patio doors provide security while shining on to the patio for dining *al fresco*. These are supplemented by dramatic lighting of focal points, such as the pond, attractive trees and the widest of the planting beds. As well as adding theatrical interest to the garden, these light up 'danger points', such as steps or ponds to help avoid night-time accidents and injury.

OUTDOOR LAMPS

Many outdoor lamps fitted to buildings are movement-activated, providing security against intruders, helping visitors find their way in the dark and helping residents to locate keys and locks. The amount of time they switch on for can be preset according to your personal requirements, from a few seconds to several minutes. There are many different styles, so choose a lamp that is in keeping with the architecture and complements the building.

LIGHT THE WAY

Outdoor lighting is far less demanding than indoor lighting when it comes to task-driven requirements. There is little call for the levels demanded for reading, stitching or other close work, but there is a need to see where you are going. This building and pathway are lit sufficiently so that no part is cast completely into darkness, but the dappled light creates an interesting, romantic feel. There is enough light to make your way to the door without stumbling, which is especially important where the pathway is uneven as here. At the door, the light is much brighter, allowing for people to see what they are doing when they put a key into the lock.

night lights

As well as permanent wired lighting, gardens can benefit from incidental lighting in the form of candles, garden flares and plug-in strings of outdoor lights. Garden flares provide dramatic lighting for pathways and bedding areas when entertaining, though you will need to keep them well away from areas where people will be gathering in groups. Many garden flares include citronella, which is a wonderfully aromatic way to deter night-time flying insects. Candles provide pretty garden lighting, and are especially effective for romantic outdoor dining. Either use them grouped in little glass holders, adding more for higher light levels, or put them inside standing or hanging hurricane lamps to protect them from being blown out by night breezes.

LIGHTING STRINGS

There is now such a plethora of decorative outdoor lighting strings that they are increasingly staying out in the garden and around the house for far longer than just the traditonal Christmas period and celebration days. Pretty little white lights in trees and shrubs, around patios and in summer houses can add a delightful decorative touch all year round. Check that the lighting strings are suitable for outdoors before you buy, then you can plug them into any outdoor socket. Also, make sure that outdoor sockets are fitted with an RCB (residual circuit breaker), a safety device that immediately cuts the supply if the cable is damaged. This is particularly important outside where cables are vulnerable to damage by electric lawnmowers and hedgecutters as well as by wildlife.

DECORATIVE GLASS

Ordinary household candle stubs give out a fairytale romantic light when placed in decorative pressed glass holders gathered together on a silver tray. Light, reflecting off the different facets and the silver tray, creates a delightful chandelier effect, increasing the amount of light that is emitted. Placing candles in glasses for use outdoors also makes sense as they are protected from the breeze, unlike naked candles. It is also a good opportunity to display the designs for appreciation at close quarters.

MARCHING LIGHT
Modern cylindrical glass candle holders, gathered together, create an almost comical crowd effect. They can be arranged randomly like this, to make a localized pool of light, or 'marched' soldier-like down pathways.

ROMANTIC LANTERNS
Unlikely raw materials of jam jars and copper foil create magical romantic lanterns. Cut a panel of copper foil to fit round each jar. Impress a design on to the panel by tracing off a motif, using a ballpoint pen. Use a bradawl or awl to pierce holes through the copper in a dotted pattern within the outline. Fix the panels round the jars with paper fasteners.

CITRONELLA CANDLES
An outdoor candle supported by an elaborate wrought-iron holder screwed to a wall illuminates a vase of dramatic flowerheads providing an exotic decorative feature for a patio. A candle this size will have many hours burning time, and the terracotta pot protects the flame from any breezes, and means it is reasonably heat-proof too. Many outdoor candles are made with citronella oil, an insect repellent extracted from a tropical lemon-scented Asian grass. These can be invaluable for evening relaxation in the garden. They smell pleasant enough to us, but their scent discourages night-flying insects, which can be so annoying after dusk

index

acknowledgements

The publishers would like to thank the following contributors for designing the projects and presenting the ideas included in this book.
Ofer Acoo: p48l. **Helen Baird:** p99br. **Fiona Barnett:** p55tr, p56t, p57tr, p55bl, p95tc, p159t, p247. **Pattie Barron:** p220b, p229bl, p232r, p244t. **Deena Beverley:** p106t, p107tr, p135tl, p152bl, p173tl, p242 (all), p243br. **Petra Boase:** p20b, p29t, p36tr, p41bl, p54bl, p111tl, p167t. **Penny Boylan:** p23br, p37bl, p40bl, p40br, p149tl, p159b, p197bl. **Shirley Bradford:** p155tr, p196b. **Rosie Brister,** Speckled Hen Cottage, 27 Chapel Street, Stoke-by-Clare. Tel: 01787 278932: p225tr. **Kathy Brown:** p194b, p245tl, p245tr. **Lisa Brown:** p14r, p36tl, p38tl. **Victoria Brown:** p49tl. **Zoe Clayton:** p39tr, p38b, p41bc. **Joan Clifton:** p220t. **Sacha Cohen:** p16b, p115br. **Karen Craggs: Anna-Lise de'Ath:** p107tl, p123tr. **Stephanie Donaldson:** p113b, p153tl, p157tl, p157br, p162t, p163bl, p168tr, p168br, p169 (all), p179r, p180r, p181bl, p183 (all), p184tl, p184bl, p192bl, p193tl, p193bl, p193br, p196tr, p198bl, p198br, p218l, p219tr, p219bl, p239r, p241tl, p246bl, p251tr, p251bl. **Marion Elliot:** p107ml, p140t, p153bl, p189bl, p235tl, p235tr, p235bl, p237br. **Tessa Evelegh:** p12tr, p12 br, p43t, p49bl, p49br, p54t, p54br, p55tl, p55bl, p56b, p57tl, p59 (all), p62 (both, p63 (both), p64 (both), p65 (all), p66 (both), p67 (both), p70 (both), p71 (both), p72br, p73bl, p73br, p74t, p75tl, p78t, p82l, p82br, p83b, p84r, p85 (all), p87tl, p87tr, p90 (both), p91 (all), p92, p93tl, p93tr, p93bl, p93br, p94t, p94bl, p95tr, p107br, p109b, p116tl, p116tr, p116br, p117t, p117bl, p118tl, p118tr, p119 (all), p121bl, p121br, p124l, p133 (all), p136t, p137b, p150tr, p161br, p164r, p165tl, p166tl, p166bl, p171 (all), p172 (all), p173tr, p173b, p187br, p191bl, p193bc, p197tl, p197br, p1998t, p199tl, p199tr, p199br, p205bl, p205br, p206l, p210t, p211 (both), p213tl, p218r, p219tr, p219bl, p221 (all), p223tl, p223tr, p223bl, p224 (both), p225bl, p227tr, p229br, p233t, p234 (both), p238l, p240, p241tr, p241br, p243br, p244b, p245b, p246tl. **Mary Fellows:** p122, p123b. **Rachel Frost:** p21t, p22l, p99bl. **Lucinda Ganderton:** p16t, p35br, p41t, p41br, p111b, p121bc, p150b, p156 (both), p158b, p168l. **Andrew Gilmore:** p125l,

p187tc. **Anna Grant:** p238r. **Celia Gregory:** p24, p25tl, p25tr. **Sandra Hatfield:** p17tl. **Karin Hossack:** p53tr, p222br, p236. **Alison Jenkins:** p49tr, p52b, p87b, p110tl, p110tr, p133l, p167b. **Dinah Kelly:** p98b. **Gilly Love:** p60r, p95b, p158t, p165br, p170 (both). **Low Wood Furnishings,** 01530 222246: p31tl. **Catherine Macdonald:** p17t. **Mary Maguire:** p53br, p124r, p125r, p239bl. **Penny Mayor:** p28 (both), p29bl, p29br. **Emma Micklethwaite:** p101tl, p192tr. **Helen Musselwhite:** p123tl, p123br. **Cleo Mussi:** p203 (both), p204, p232l, p243tl. **Andrew Newton-cox:** p402 (all). **Gloria Nichols:** p42l, p43b, p94br, p95tl, p162br, p250. **Harumi Nishi:** p22r, p45, p47tr, p47bl, p93bc, p195. **Jenny Norton:** p215tr, p215bl. **Deirdre O'Malley:** p53br. **Sandra Partington:** p35tr. **Maggie Philo:** p99t, p128. **Maggie Pryce:** p184br. **Tabby Riley:** p25b. **Kim Rowley:** p157bl. **Michael Savage:** p48tr. **Kerry Skinner, Rare Creation:** p53tl. **Judy Smith:** p15bl, p131b, p189t. **Andrea Spencer:** p18l, p23tr, p23bl, p26tr, p32 (both), p33br, p40tr, p42bl, p60l, p61 (both), p68 (both), p69 (both), P72bl, p73t, p74b, p75tr, p75c, p75b, p76 (all), p77 (all), p78b, p79 (all), p80 (all), p81 (all), p82tr, p83t, p84l, p86t, p86bl, p100r, p101tr, p101b, p102r, p104 (both), p106b, p107bl, p110bl, p112r, p116bl, p133tr, p133br, p134 (both), p136b, p139t, p143b, p198r, p148, p154 (both), p155b, p166tr, p178br, p179tl, p179bl, p182tl, p182bl, p188 (both), p187tl, p187tr, p190 (both), p191tl, p191br, p196tl, p233bl, p233br. **Lesley Stanfield:** p161bl. **Isabel Stanley:** p19t, p20tl, p20tr, p23tr, p26b, p39 (both), p135tr, p135br, p135bl, p137tr, p152lr, p153br. **Catherine Tully:** p15tl, p31tr, p58 (both), p147br. **Liz Wagstaff:** p17br, p27 (all), p40tl, p48br, p98tr, p0214, p223br. **Stewart and Sally Walton:** p14l, p15tr, p15br, p26tl, p31b, p72t, p98tl, p102l, p103 (all), p108 (both), p109t, p111tr, p112 (all), p113tl, p113tr, p114l, p115tl, p117br, p129 (both), p130, p131tl, p131tr, p138l, p139b, p151tr, p157tr, p161tr, p176b, p177bl, 177br, p181tr, p182tr, p185 (both), p187bl, p188 (both), p189br, p222l. **Josephine Whitfield:** p115bl, p137tl. **Dorothy Wood:** p12l, p18r, p19b, p21bl, p21br, p30 (both), p33tl, p33tr, p33bl, p34 (both), p35tl, p35b, p36tr, p142 (both), p198l, p199, p149tr, p149bl, p149br, p150tl, p151tl, p151bl, p152tl, p153tr, p155tl, p180l, p181br. **Diana Yakeley:** p13 (both), p44 (all), p46 (all), p47tl, p47br, p86br, p88 (both), p89, p100l, p105 (both), p118br, p120, p121tl, p121tr, p138r, p140b, p141t, p143t, p146 p147t, p147bl, p160, p161tl, p164l, p165bl, p176tl, p176tr, p177t, p194tl, p194tr. **Daniella Zimmerman:** p37t.

The publishers would like to thank the following garden owners, designers and institutions for allowing their gardens to be included in this book.
Brook Hall (designers: Prof. Keith Hopkins and Dr. Jennifer Hopkins): p208l. **Chelsea Flower Show 1998:** p215tl. **Chelsea Flower Show 1999:** p202b 'Help the Aged World Life Garden' (designer: Naila Green); p212br; p212bl, p227tl 'Mr McGregor's Garden' (designer: Jacquie Gordon); p226t '21st century street' (designer: Carol Klein); p228t 'My

Retreat' (designer: Andrew Bond). **The Coppice,** Reigate, Surrey: p209t. **Fairweather Sculpture,** Hillside House, Startston, Norfolk (garden designer and sculptor: Dennis Fairweather): p222tr. **Forge Cottage,** Jaspers Green (designer: Carolynn Blythe): p239l. **Fovant Hut,** Witshire (designer: Christina Oates): p212tr. **The Garden in Mind,** Hampshire (designer: Ivan Hicks): p225br. **Hampton Court Flower Show, 1999:** p207br, p208l 'A Safe Haven Garden' (designer: Ruth Chivers). **Hampton Court Flower Show, 2001:** p231tl. **The Hannah Peschar Sculpture Garden,** Black and White Cottage, Ockley, Surrey (designed by Anthony Paul, Landscaper Designer): p205t 'Sit' by Hannar Peschar; p226b 'Pictish Spiral Bench' by Nigel Ross; p237tl 'Amongst words and phrases' by Mark Clayne Frith. **The Heatley Garden,** Takapuna, New Zealand (designer: Margaret Phillips and Michael Poulgrain): p249tl. **Iford Manor,** Bradford-upon-Avon, Wiltshire: p213tr, p219br. **Little Cottage,** Lymington: p209b. **Beverley Mills,** London: p237tr. **Leeann Roots** (owner and designer): p251tl. **Tatton Park, RHS Flower Show, 1999:** p215br 'Oasis in the Urban Jungle' (designer: Jan Williams). **Tatton Park, RHS Flower Show, 2000:** p237tc. **Tatton Park, RHS Flower Show, 2001:** p228b, p231b 'Living Edge'/John Lewis Garden (designer: Butler Landscapes Design and Construction. butler.landscapes@virgin.net). **Julian van den Bosch's garden,** Ham, London: p237br. **West Green House Garden,** near Hartney, Wintney, Hampshire: p217bl. **Sumil Wickes** garden, London (designer: Lara Copley-Smith): p230, p248, p249r. **Winkle Howarth Garden:** p231tr. **Diane Yakeley** (garden designer), 13 College Cross, Islington, London: p227b.

The Publishers would also like to thank the following photographers for taking the images.
Craft and Lifestyle: Caroline Arber, Norio Asai, Paul Bricknell, Nicki Dowey, Polly Eltes, Rodney Forte, John Freeman, Michelle Garrett, Tim Imrie, James Mitchell, Gloria Nichol, Harumi Nishi, Lizzie Orme, David Parmiter, Debbie Patterson, Spike Powell, Graham Rae, Russel Sadur, Lucinda Symons, Adrian Taylor, Peter Williams, Polly Wreford.
Gardening: Peter Anderson, Jonathan Buckley, Sarah Cottell, Michelle Garrett, Simon McBride, Marie O'Hara, Debbie Patterson, Jo Whitworth, Steven Wooster.